A DECLARATION OF WAR

Screaming Wolf

Table Of Contents

Preface from the original editors

A MESSAGE FROM THE UNDERGROUND

My husband and I are animal rights activists. For the past ten years we have been in trenches fighting for the animals. But we have always fought legally. We have used the system to its fullest, coordinating various educational, legislative, and litigious campaigns.

If you would have asked us how we felt about our work, we would have told you that our struggle for animal rights and a more humane world was finally becoming mainstream and acceptable. We really believed that our message was beginning to be heard.

However, on the morning of January 18, 1991, our lives were turned upside down.

Included in our mail was a small package with no return address. Inside was a computer disk. There was no explanation of what this disk was for, or who had sent it to us. We looked at the postmark on the envelope, but it was faint and illegible. With no clues as to its contents, we decided to put it in our computer and see what was on it.

The disk had one file on it called: "A Declaration of War." We opened the file, and the following message appeared:

This manuscript explains the philosophy of a group of individuals throughout the world who call themselves, 'Liberators.' They believe in a revolution to liberate animals and, if necessary, to kill their oppressors. They say such extreme action is needed to stop the horrible human caused suffering of animals and the destruction of the world. They believe that nothing short of a total overthrow of this system will free our brothers and sisters. Please see that this 'Declaration of War' is published for the world to read and understand. Signed - Screaming Wolf

Our curiosity kept us glued to the computer for the next four hours, as we read this bold manuscript. When we finished, we were extremely disturbed. What kind of person could be responsible for this, we wondered. At first, we couldn't understand why we were chosen as the recipients of this 'Declaration of War.' After thinking it through, we assumed it was because of some similarities in our personal philosophies. We, too, see humans as the destructive force in the world. We feel that this planet was not put here for humans to exploit, and that nature and other animals, not humans, are at the center of our moral thinking.

But what was this talk of killing oppressors? We never promoted or defended violence. Why did Screaming Wolf decide to contact us? The answer to that question is still a mystery, But the reason for our selection is a moot point. We have been selected and must now deal with this terrifying manuscript.

Screaming Wolf explains the reason why 'Liberators' feel that they must declare war on society. We expect that many activists in the animal rights and environmental movements agree with much of what the 'Liberators' have to say, but would seldom admit these deep and frightening thoughts, even to themselves. Feelings of frustration, feelings of alienation, feelings of love and hate and anger and fear, all of these, and more, are common to all of us working within the system for change.

However, the 'Liberators' go beyond these feelings, and describe real or proposed actions: actions which the public will immediately decry as terrorism, actions which the 'Liberators' defend as heroism. According to Screaming Wolf, who apparently is a spokesperson for these 'Liberators,' these terrorists are a branch of the A.L.F. (Animal Liberation Front). This group has claimed responsibility for breaking into laboratories and factory farms, rescuing animals and damaging equipment. However, the A.L.F. has maintained a commitment of nonviolence towards all living beings, including humans. Liberators, according to Screaming Wolf, have decided to end their commitment of non-violence towards human life. These people actually feel that violence against humans is the only way to make a real difference for the animals.

After reading this manuscript, our anxiety and fear almost prompted us to toss it in trash. We were looking for any excuse to forget what we had just read. However, we concluded that Screaming Wolf's message is too important to simply dismiss. People must know what 'Liberators' believe, and can come to their own conclusions about what it means, how they feel about it, and what they want to do about it.

We know that publishing a book like this is risky, despite the alleged First Amendment rights of freedom of press. People in this country are allowed to purchase and bear arms, but not to announce a call to arms. We expect some people to construe our publication of this book as an endorsement of violence, despite our disclaimers to the contrary. We looked into the laws regarding publication of literature concerning terrorism and realized at once that the risk in publishing this book is real. We expect to be slapped with dozens of lawsuits, and probably death threats as well. As one lawyer put it, our publishing this book may be totally legally defensible, but we will most likely have to repeatedly prove that fact over the next decade, costing us a fortune in legal fees, and draining our energy and time as we deal with the legal system.

The situation, as we see it, is that we have been the recipients of a manuscript that describes a terrorist group of people declaring war on humans to save animals and the environment. If we ignore the manuscript, the public will not know of this threat to its safety. People need to know that 'Liberators' exist. We also feel that everyone who believes in working within the system needs to engage in open and honest dialogue about all ways of seeing a problem and its possible solutions, including the solution offered by the 'Liberators.' This applies to activists and those invested in the status quo. The message of 'Liberators' affects all of these people.

We concluded, therefore, that we must accept the responsibility of publishing this manuscript. In the name of truth and honesty, people must hear this message of the 'Liberators.'

In an attempt to protect ourselves from criminal prosecution, we, the publishers, would like to make the following direct disclaimer. **We do not endorse or support any of the illegal, terrorist activities described by Screaming Wolf or the 'Liberators.'**

We present this book for informational purposes only.

The entire manuscript of Screaming Wolf could have been printed with quotation marks from the first word to the last, since all that follows this preface are the words of that individual and his or her presentation of the 'Liberator' position. We have excluded such quotation marks for the purpose of clarity.

This is a glimpse into the world of animal liberation terrorism. We suspect that the life and message of a 'Liberator' will be a difficult one for most people to understand. But we feel that the public has a right to have this information. After all, if the 'Liberators' continue to carry out their tactics, it may be a matter of life and death.

The Publishers
February, 1991

MAJOR DISCLAIMER
by Screaming Wolf

This book describes the opinions and feelings of a group of people who were once members of the Animal Liberation Front.

They have broken off from the Animal Liberation Front and now support the use of violence against humans to save animals. It is my, Screaming Wolf's, understanding that the law considers animals to be property, not persons.

Only persons are protected under the law. Killing people to save animals, then, would be completely unacceptable and unjustifiable under the laws of this land. I have been told that it is illegal to support terrorism against humans in the name of freeing animals.

I, Screaming Wolf, would never commit an illegal act or encourage others to do so.

The discerning reader may find places where I clearly agree with liberators, particularly concerning human nature and the nature of societies. However, all statements that even remotely sound terrorist are the liberators', not my own.

Chapter One

THE LIBERATORS

Who are the liberators? What events have transformed these compassionate animal defenders into terrorists?

My reason for writing this book is to let the public know why groups like the Animal Liberation Front, or A.L.F., and eco-saboteurs exist. What possibly possesses people to become so extreme that they are willing to engage in terrorist activities for the cause of saving animals and the planet on which they live?

Animal abusers have already felt the effect of actions directed against property. A.L.F. raids are notorious for their success in freeing animals, destroying property used in animal abuse, while maintaining a position of nonviolence to all life, including humans. A fire at University of California at Davis destroyed an unfinished animal research building, causing almost $5 million in damage.

However, **extremists are extending such activities, from destroying property used in the murder and torture of animals, to attacking the real causes of the abuse: people.**

This issue is clearly important, given the recent car bombing in England of an animal researcher's vehicle. These activities have begun in the United States with the attempted assassination of the president of U.S. Surgical Corporation, a business that demonstrates surgical staples on dogs. And some eco-saboteurs do equally extreme acts to end what they regard as the raping of the planet by logging companies, mining companies, and other "natural resource" exploiters.

I must explain what this book is not about. This is not an attempt to convince you why animals should have their freedom respected. Liberators don't believe anyone can use words to convince others of moral principles, as explained later. You either believe that we are all animals with an equal claim to life and that human animals must respect those claims, or you believe that humans are non-animals, special beings who have every right to use others as they wish.

Liberators believe that a human has a no greater claim to life than a mole or a sea bass. They feel that humans are the lowest form of life, and that the world would be a much better, more peaceful place without them. If you agree with this position, then you will love this book.

If you believe that humans are the chosen species or the highest point of biological evolution, and that this somehow gives them a right to abuse other creatures, then this book is important to you, too. **It will let you**

know that you are a target for animal liberators. Every time you abuse another creature, look over your shoulder. Through liberators, the animals are now fighting back.

There are some of you who locate yourselves between these extreme positions. You believe that animals should be treated well, but you still place humans on a throne. Conflicted by your empathy for other creatures and your need for control, you play the moderate. You try cooling down extremist animal defenders, calling for nonviolence and dialogue, and you try increasing the sensitivity of animal abusers, calling for larger cages and "humane slaughter". You will find this book disturbing. According to liberators, **there is no room for moderation and compromise when it comes to moral principles concerning life and death. And liberators are concerned with life and death.**

To give you an idea of who these liberators are as people, I will trace the development of an average person into a liberator.

There was a time in the lives of liberators when they would have killed an animal to save a human. And they would have thought nothing about loggers cutting roads into virgin timberland.

At one time, they weren't even aware that the food on their plates was once an animal. They gave no thought to wearing fur or leather, and enjoyed seeing animals behind bars in zoos. While they always loved animals, they still regarded human life as more valuable and worthy than non-human life.

Yet, despite their socially programmed bias for human animals, liberators found themselves more comfortable in the company of squirrel's and birds than people. Like most people, they lived the contradiction of abusing other beings while at the same time loving them.

Liberators, after all, are human. Humans have a great capacity for fooling themselves. We feel one way, but think another. We feel that animals should be free to live their own lives, but we think that such freedom would unreasonably conflict with our lifestyles. We like drugs, and meat, and other products of animal exploitation, but we feel sick when we learn exactly what happens to the animals during the production of such products. That's why slaughter houses are out of public view, and research lab doors are kept closed. It helps people keep their heads in the sand, closing their eyes to all the cruelty around them. Some people turn off their feelings to suffering animals, and fabricate ideas to justify their acts of animal abuse. Society supports this, since it values thoughts over feelings. These people learn to suppress what they really feel when they see animals suffering.

Separating thoughts from feelings is a part of the process of alienation that plagues humankind.

Because if this alienation, most people have no sense of where they belong in the world, or who they themselves really are. Pop psychology and self-help books overflow on the shelves of bookstores, as these confused, frightened, and lonely people seek help from pieces of paper, hoping to put some meaning and love in their lives. But it takes more than words to change people's lives and re-integrate alienated humans into a balanced, natural world. Despite the encouraging writings of self-appointed gurus, their abuse of animals, and of themselves, continues. These people never become liberators.

The people who do become liberators examine personal feelings and thoughts, and discard ideas that don't fit the world in which they want to live. **They realize that ideas are no more than justifications of feelings. Getting in touch with their feelings** helps them avoid the alienation that leads to so much human pain and suffering. As they keep in touch with their feelings, they abandon animal abuse, and transform their way of life into a more compassionate one.

They then join support groups. They join out of a sense of helplessness and a growing need to do something, to change the world. They sometimes fight with old friends who still support animal research or hunting, while trying to find new friends. Meanwhile, they adopt a vegetarian lifestyle, since they don't believe in eating their nonhuman friends. This makes them social pariahs, and even their families can't wait until they get through this new "phase" that they are in.

After a few years, the "phase" is considered an unhealthy obsession. They are taking this animal issue to extremes, they are told. **Nobody likes extremists.** Extremists take their beliefs seriously and practice them consistently. **Most people are frightened by consistency. It takes too much work.** As a result, friends are not as easy to locate as before. The problem is that they begin to feel comfortable only with other animal "extremists," and such people tend to like animals more than they like people.

There is a reason why people who become liberators turn to animals for affection. **There is an honesty about non-humans. They don't play games. They are direct. And they are never intentionally cruel.**

Eventually, they grow frustrated as their efforts for saving animals seem impotent in making a big difference. They get donation pitches in the mail each week from animal welfare and animal rights organizations, telling them how much the organizations have done for the animals, how much still needs to be done, how the opposition is mounting a counter-offensive, and how little money there is to fight back and preserve whatever advances have been made. **They ask themselves whether these organizations, some with millions of dollars in investments and executive directors earning six figure incomes, have become permanent institutions in our cruel society, more invested in maintaining the status quo than in freeing animals.**

They start questioning whether animal abuse will ever stop given current approaches. Basic beliefs come under scrutiny, as they examine whether humans can ever be the agents for liberating animals. Questions like, "Can we ever change the system from within?" pop into their minds. And for the first time, they do not answer automatically in the affirmative. They reflect on their feelings about people, society, animals, and the way things have been done in the past. **They begin to even wonder if the concept of animal "rights" is what the animals really need.**

These increasingly frustrated individuals examine their assumption that educating the public about what is really happening to the animals will somehow lead to the termination of the cruelty. That assumption demands a faith in the fairness and compassion of human nature that these people no longer take on face value. **They begin to question whether showing people movies and photos of monkeys with electrodes in their heads, or wolves caught by steel-jaw leghold traps, or calves immobilized in dark, claustrophobic veal crates, or chickens crowded and stressed by factory farm conditions, will motivate the common person to change their consumption patterns and other abusive behaviors.**

At one time, the common person would hunt, slaughter, skin, and beat animals as a regular part of life. It is an illusion of contemporary society that people today are more compassionate than in that cruel past. Actually, the general public has simply become unaccustomed to killing animals themselves. The dirty work is left to "specialists," like butchers, trappers, animal researchers, and animal shelter workers.

History has shown, however, that **humans have an enormous capacity to revert to barbaric behavior at the first sign of potential personal gain.** The same insensitivity that allows "specialists" to kill would allow the average person to kill, as well. At the current time, this insensitivity allows people to be comfortable in the knowledge that others are doing the killing for them. **If people today are sensitive to pictures of animal abuse, then the interest people have in the products of that abuse will simply cause them to turn away from the pictures, or to accept that such acts against animals are "a necessary evil".**

So these developing liberators conclude that, in the long run, showing the public pictures of animal abuse will only further desensitize people to animal suffering. **Humans can adapt to all assaults to their sensibilities, especially when they are committed to certain behaviors.**

They then try to appeal to the public, legislators, product manufacturers, and others in power, through letter writing, boycotts, rallies, demonstrations, and marches. But their efforts get them nowhere. Every small victory is challenged. Despite years of lobbying and writing to Congressmen, the only major legislation passed in recent history for animal protection was the Federal Animal Welfare Act, designed primarily to protect animals exploited in research. Yet, before the ink could dry on the new legislation, animal abusers clamored to water down its already compromised and weakened impact.

As a result of lobbying by animal abusers, farm animals are exempt from the act, as are rodents. When you consider that about 90% of animal research is done on rodents, it's easy to see that the effect of the Act on animal suffering is minimal. Further, any acts of terror can be committed against any and all animals in the name of research, so long as it is deemed "necessary" for the research project. Since farm animals are exempt from the Act, many researchers now target pigs and sheep as totally unprotected subjects. **It's hard to keep a cruel researcher down!**

The increasingly angry animal defenders passionately hold onto their dubious victories to convince themselves that those victories are substantial and meaningful. They demand to legislators that the Act is enforced, a difficult task since the Department of Agriculture, which is responsible for its enforcement, has too few inspectors, and too little interest, in doing its job. **This leads these soon-to-be liberators to the sad realization that laws are only as good as the intent to obey them.**

Recognizing these failures, they look to other signs of success to bolster their optimism. We see that vegetarianism is more acceptable than before, with more vegetarians in this country than in the past. Further examination reveals that many so called "vegetarians" eat fish and poultry. Almost all of these "vegetarians" eat dairy and/or eggs, which is merely exchanging solid flesh for liquid flesh.

At most, only 3% of the population say they are "vegetarians". When we consider a population of 270,000,000 people, 3% seems a great amount of vegetarians, surely enough to generate a market for special products and magazines. But there are still 262,000,000 people eating animal flesh, and the numbers of animals killed for food continues to increase. Put differently, 97 out of every 100 babies born in this country are being raised as flesh eaters.

They turn their attention to the fur issue, an area where they can feel certain success. After all fur is no longer a fashionable commodity. Unfortunately, they discover that fur stores have opened up in Asian countries, so that the industry has simply generated new markets to replace the old ones it has lost. They also learn that fur is unfashionable primarily in the United States and England, but is still popular in some European countries. And knowing how fashions come and go, these people, increasingly anxious about making a difference for the animals, develop a uneasiness over the current fur taboo, wondering when fur will again become a desirable commodity.

Finally, they turn their attention to cosmetic and household product testing on animals. Feeling certain that the general public will never sanction such blatant animal abuse, they boycott the companies selling these products of death. When some of the companies agree to stop animal testing, the animal lovers rejoice at the news. They feel vindicated in their approach of working within the system and fighting with their pocketbooks.

To maintain their feeling of success, however, they try to ignore the fact that many of the companies, who say they no longer use animal tests, are farming out the tests to other companies, or are buying animal tested ingredients from suppliers to use in their allegedly cruelty free product line.

Eventually, they begin to realize that fighting for the animals is like trying to put out thousands of brush fires. Tremendous effort and time is spent focusing on one fire, which may or may not be extinguished, while ten others are being started. It is a never ending battle fighting this way. And it is a losing proposition.

Eventually, these animal extremists step back from the smoky field, and reflect on the causes of the fires. If they can eliminate some of the causes, they conclude, then they wouldn't have to fight so many flames.

In short, these people move towards greater and greater extremism as they find all their efforts to help the animals frustrated by the abusive system with which they are fighting. They examine and question all their assumptions and approaches, and for once they feel that they are really beginning to get in touch with the depth of the problem, and with possible solutions. Finally, they come up with bold, revolutionary ideas. **In fact, they conclude that a revolution is essential for freeing the animals.**

Let me summarize this conclusion of people who have come to call themselves animal liberators. It will be direct, challenging, uncompromising, and frightening to all animal abuser and others invested in the system.

Liberators believe in killing humans to save animals!

If an animal researcher said: "It's a dog or a child," a liberator will defend the dog every time. A liberator also believes that disposing of a few researchers will save even more dogs from their cruelty.

Liberators have come to one unavoidable conclusion: **HUMANS WILL NEVER MAKE PEACE WITH ANIMALS! It is not in their natures or in the natures of the societies they have created. In fact, liberators believe that if people really want to save the animals, they must stop wasting their time trying to improve the human race and its societies. They must declare war against humans. They must join in this revolution!**

Liberators believe this is the only logical, consistent, and morally correct conclusion stemming from a true belief that animals should be free to live their lives unshackled from human exploitation. **They believe that the nature of human society and its laws are implicitly and irrevocably immoral. Liberators are people of conscience who feel morally obligated to break those laws and revolt against this oppressive regime.**

But this revolution by liberators will not be like any other in the history of the world.

Normally, revolutions seek to gain privileges within society for a disenfranchised group of people. The civil rights movement, for example, was dedicated to gaining protection and enforcement of those rights blacks were assured in the Constitution since the Civil War. **It was a movement for inclusion in society.** The same thing goes for the gay rights movement, or the feminist movement.

The liberation movement to end animal exploitation is nothing like these others, as the liberators see it. And according to them, this difference has made the struggle for freedom for animals, as it has been practiced to this day, to be nothing more than an impotent whimper in the face of gross inhumanity.

Liberators feel this movement demands a different approach because human groups fight for inclusion. The movement to free animals must fight for exclusion. Oppressed people want to be accepted as equals into society. Oppressed animals want to be left alone by society.[1]

This difference, according to liberators, dictates different strategies for the animal rights activist than for any other social reformer. For one thing, it makes non-violent tactics, as modeled by Gandhi or King, inappropriate.

Liberators believe that only physical harm will dissuade people from abusing animals.

Their message is not simply that we should shoot hunters, kill vivisectors, trap trappers, and butcher butchers in order to free the animals. They believe we are morally justified in doing these things, and that we must do it to free some animals. But liberators do not believe that it will change the world and result in the freedom of all animals.

Liberators hold that nothing will result in the freedom of all animals, short of the extinction of human species. People will abuse other creatures so long as the human species exists. This is an observation liberators base on human nature, and they believe human nature is not about to change. Liberators are not simply pessimists in making this statement. To them, it is a realistic appraisal of the history of human blood lust and speciesism. It is their bold acceptance of what they feel many people really know deep in their hearts. But liberators expect few people will acknowledge what they feel in their hearts. Who wants to accept the fact that their efforts and hopes are useless?

The liberators feel it's time for animal defenders, and those concerned about the environment, to open their eyes and admit that they shall never overcome.

In short, the liberators believe that history has shown that working within the cruel system and winning small battles for the animals will soon prove irrelevant. The carnage against animals continues. The opposition is stronger, better financed, and more numerous than animal defenders. Gains made are easily reversed. Animal abuse will go on until mankind becomes extinct, or the planet is destroyed.

According to this extremist position, it follows that people who want to help the animals must not use their energy trying to change the system – that's impossible. They must focus their efforts on rescuing as many animals as they can and give animal abusers as much trouble as possible – they must be liberators of animals! The purpose of this revolution would not be to discard the old powers and put in the new. According to the liberator philosophy, **no human system will ever treat animals with respect.** The animals simply need a continuous revolution to consistently, repeatedly, and uncompromisingly liberate them from human oppression. They need a revolution against human society because it is intrinsically oppressive. **So long as there are people, animals will need this revolution.**

Liberators believe a technique called **militant interventionism** is a necessary measure for animal liberation, given the natures of society and people. Liberators believe that working within the system will never work for the animals, and that non-violent resistance is completely inappropriate for the animal liberation movement. In this book, I will explain their reasons for these conclusions.

I will also give some examples of how they might try to monkey wrench the system. And I will explain how these individuals, dedicated to this revolution, committed to sabotage, believe that they can still find love and peace in their lives.

----

1. According to Liberators, the need for exclusion from human society applies to all animals exploited by humans, including wild life and animals raised for food, research, entertainment, or any other human defined purpose. It also includes domesticated household animals, such as dogs and cats, who have had their spirits genetically broken, since they have been bred to be dependent on humans. They live on human terms, in human communities, and are trained to suppress any remnants of their natural instincts. They are slaves who have become dependent on their slavery. A further discussion of the "pet" problem is near the end of this book.

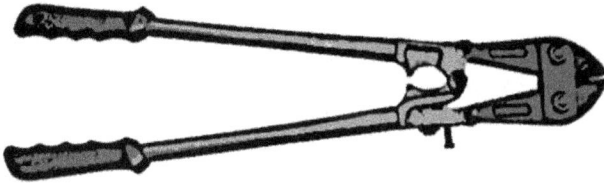

Chapter Two

THIS WORLD IS MEANT FOR ALL BEINGS

THIS WORLD IS MEANT FOR ALL BEINGS
To make clear their position regarding animals, liberators make the following statement :

"ALL BEINGS ARE EQUAL! HUMANS DESERVE NO SPECIAL PRIVILEGES OR CONSIDERATION. IN FACT, HUMANS ARE THE ONLY CREATURES WITH THE CAPACITY FOR EVIL."

Non-human animals are living, feeling beings entitled to enjoy their own lives as they see fit, free from human interference. Non-humans are sentient, which means they are conscious of their interests and needs and whether or not they are fulfilled. Humans have no right to interfere with other creatures as they try to fulfill their needs, just as we expect to be free to fulfill our own.

Liberators believe that environmental issues are connected to animal issues. They feel this connection should be obvious. If you respect animals, then you must respect their homes. Cutting down a tree destroys part of the living space of other creatures. In some cases, it is the home of many other beings, such as birds, small mammals, and insects. Of course, liberators know that there is a reason why people cut down trees. They believe it is because people see the world as a "natural resource," as a means to human ends.

As a liberator sees it, the world has been defined by man to be for man. Placing man at the center of the world is called **anthropocentrism**. It allows humans to regard animals as "natural resources," objects for human use and consumption. These self-serving notions are even glorified in religious writings, such as the Bible, imbuing these violent practices with alleged divine acceptance, and insulating them from reflection by erecting impenetrable walls of faith. **Bloodthirsty humans need little justification for their massacre of nature, but armed with faith they are a non-stoppable, self-promoting holocaust.**

This anthropocentric view of the world has also resulted in environmental destruction. Mountains, rivers, and even entire rainforests are nothing more than objects to satisfy man's hunger for control and material possessions. And this subjugation of the world and its inhabitants to human desires has not exempted people from slaughtering one another, as well. This is because the connection between non-humans and humans is irrefutable. We are all animals. If non-human animals are exploitable and expendable, then so are human animals.

Anthropocentrism is similar to egocentrism. When someone behaves as though he or she is the only person whose interests and needs mattered, we call that person self-centered, or egocentric. Such a person thinks nothing about the needs of others. The world and all its inhabitants are there for his or her amusement and use. Analogously, when people think of humans as the only beings who matter, we can call those people human-centered, or anthropocentric. Both egocentrism and anthropocentrism result in abuse of others, since they are self-serving perspectives. In fact, **all egocentric people are also anthropocentric.** To them, the world is for their use. These egocentric people, who see themselves as the center of the human world, will see humans as the center of the natural world.

The reverse is not true, however. Many people consider themselves altruistic lovers of mankind, willing to die on the cross as their hero, Christ, had done to atone for man's sinfulness. These people would not be considered egocentric. Yet, they put the interests and needs of humans at the highest priority. They put mankind on a pedestal over all other creatures, and consider the world to be man's resource base. Liberators believe that **the saints of mankind are still the sinners of the world.**

Using this line of thinking, liberators conclude that anthropocentrism alienates humans from the rest of the natural world. Anthropocentric people consider humans separate from nature and the environment, a reality experienced by millions of people living in asphalt and cement cities. In most cities, nature is limited to urban landscape designs, where an occasional tree is planted in a cement pot or in a small opening in the sidewalk. The only feature of the natural world left untouched is the weather, although people hide in their environmentally controlled buildings to minimize this affect of nature on their lives.

When anthropocentric people feel affection for animals or nature, their feelings are always tainted by their human-centeredness. When they say they love animals, they mean they like animals for what they offer people. Usually, they prefer domestic animals. Domestication is a process whereby animals are bred for human manipulation and control. **Dogs, cats, and other "pets" are objects of affection for people who think about animal life in relation to human needs.**

When it comes to loving nature, these people see the great outdoors as a rejuvenating getaway from urban life. They enjoy the tall trees, clean air, and clean rivers and lakes. They value the way nature makes them feel. They believe in saving a forest, because they like to hike in them. They plead for saving a particular river, because they like to fish in it. They cry for saving the rainforests, because **their** planet depends on it.

Rainforests, in fact, are a primary concern for anthropocentric enviro-nmentalists for many reasons that reveal their human-centered bias.

Besides the greenhouse effect resulting from rainforest destruction, they complain that species of plants and animals are becoming extinct as the forests are destroyed. Why is that important? It is because we way lose potentially beneficial medicinal plants. Also, loss of animal species reduces the world's gene pool and **robs humans** of rich, varied biological resources. They do not care about the lives of individual animals. All they care about is endangered species, and the effect of such a loss on humans.

The anthropocentric perspective has led environmentalists and animal defenders to be at odds with one another. These animal lovers care more about cats and dogs than about redwoods, while these environmentalists care more about keeping the wild available for human recreational use than about animals. Such environmentalists support the practice of adding animals to wildlife areas, as the state Fish and "Game"2 Departments do, to sustain the population at a level that will allow hunters to have fun killing animals every season.

The anthropocentric approach makes animal and environmental issues seem like two separate issues. This is no surprise. Alienated people, who are themselves apart from nature, see animals unconnected to their environments, as well.

Liberators see things differently. They see the environment as an integration of beings with their surroundings. Animals are extensions of the trees, rivers, grasses, rain, snow, earth, air, clouds, and all of the planet. The entire planet is one system. And the whole of the planet is greater than the sum of its animal, vegetable, and mineral parts. To separate animals from the environment is a human mental construct. It has nothing to do with reality.

All animals and plants come from the earth. They all return to the earth. They are composed of the same ingredients. They are different manifestations of the same oneness of the world.

To live by this view, liberators have adopted a naturocentric ethic, in which they see the human place in the world from the perspective of the entire natural world. This view sees humans, not as the center of the planet, but only as one participant among a majority of others. **Man is not even the most important participant. Why should he be? Elephants, otters, sea bass, spiders, and vultures have as much a right to be on this planet as humans.**

A naturocentric view is holistic. As such, it joins the animal and environmental movements into one movement of liberation of the world from human tyranny and exploitation. Liberators believe they must care for the environment, not because it has value to humans, but because it is the home of their non-human brothers and sisters.

To liberators, having an animal movement without a defense of the environment is absurd. Animals need a place to live, and a destruction of the environment is actually a destruction of the animals.

To have an environmental movement without a primary concern for animals is nothing more than human self-centeredness. To be concerned about the environment without a concern for its animal component is to see the environment only on human terms.

Only with a naturocentric ethic can animal lovers and environmentalists come together to combat human oppression of others and the destruction of the world. This naturocentric ethic considers environmentalism a component of the animal movement. Liberators care about the environment because it is where their brothers and sisters live. The animals are their environment. Defending the environment is defending the animals.

By considering environmental protection an animal issue, liberators are not suggesting that such life forms as trees don't matter. They certainly do matter. They believe that the more we get in touch with our natures as animals, the more we can feel a connection to all life forms. We can stand next to a tree and feel its life force and strength. A naturocentric ethic focuses on such connection.

When a tree is cut down, we feel part of ourselves destroyed. Our connection has been severed. This feeling of a loss of connection is what motivates liberators to respect trees and other aspects of the environment of which they are a part. They defend the environment, therefore, as they defend themselves and the other creatures connected to it.

For liberators, **environmental defense is an extension of animal defense**. If no animals were connected to or affected by an environment, it wouldn't matter what happened to it. **Environments matter when they are the fountainheads of living beings to whom life matters**. This is another way of saying that the environmental movement is a subsidiary of the animal movement.

A liberators' commitment to non-human animals is deeper than mere lip service. They have a spiritual connection with all beings, a feeling of oneness with all of creation. What happens to the armadillo being, or the deer being, or the dove being affects liberators, since they are the liberators' family and loved ones. These other beings are the liberators' brothers and sisters, and the liberators treat them with respect, integrity, and loyalty. And when they say that the other beings are their family, they mean that they will defend them as they would their blood brothers and sisters.

Loving animals, for a liberator, is more than getting pleasure playing with a puppy or kitten. It's a commitment to respect animal beings in all personal actions, and to stand by them to fight all humans who would oppress them.

Many people proclaim a love for animals. Hunters say they love wildlife, even as they empty their semiautomatic weapons into anything that moves. Trappers insist they love animals, too, and maintain that the leghold traps they use are not excessively painful to the animals unlucky enough to be crunched by them. Even animal researchers boast a love for animals, and insist that the tortures they submit our brothers and sisters to are necessary for human health.

The self-serving, human centered beliefs of hunters, trappers, and researchers should be obvious even to people disinterested in animals. But to liberators, some alleged "animal lovers," and even members of "humane" organizations, are equally laughable in their view of animals. These alleged animal defenders and lovers are hypocrites, as liberators see it. They still consider animals objects for human exploitation. Only, please, exploit them in a humane way, these hypocrites ask. Torturing and killing animals in laboratories is justified if it is for "necessary" research, provided it is done with compassion. Even eating animals is acceptable, so long as they are "humanely slaughtered".

To liberators, who see animals as family, the concept of "humane slaughter," for any cause, is a perversity. It shows how confused humans are in what it means to be humane. Humane slaughter is an oxymoron, like military intelligence. **Liberators feel that killing an innocent being, human or non-human, who does not want to die, is never humane.**

The example liberators use is the following. Would you ever regard the murder of your brother or sister as humane? What if the murderer pleaded with you that he killed your sister lovingly, with an overdose of barbiturates, or with electrocution? Would you smile and agree that her murder was humane?

Liberators believe that the real reason for calling animal slaughter "humane" is that it makes the process easier for the killers. Making murder easy for people is what liberators say many "humane" organizations are all about. They point out that 15 million dogs and cats are killed in "shelters" every year. The public doesn't want to think that their unwanted pets are being killed with two-by-fours crashed over their skulls. **It is more humane to people to kill the animals more discretely**, say, by injection. Never mind that the destroyed animals are murdered for no other reason than human negligence and unwillingness to change the system, like shutting down pet shops, making breeding illegal, and mandating neutering.

Liberators are disgusted with many animal and environmental defense groups who have fat bank accounts, and who willingly accept that they will probably never change the system. Some of these organizations have existed for over 100 years. Meanwhile, animal abuse has grown steadily.

Do these organizations reflect on the obvious inadequacy of their approach? No, exclaim the liberators! They simply look ahead to the next 100 years of working within the system.

Liberators scoff at people who beat their chests in defense of animal welfare, and even some who say they believe in animals rights, but who have no problem with the killing of animals. These people oppose the suffering of animals, not their murder. They are against factory farming, where animals are treated as machines and are confined to dark, limited, overcrowded spaces. Yet, they have no objection to killing animals for food if the creatures are raised on old fashioned family farms before the slaughter. So long as the animals are treated well while alive, there is nothing wrong with killing them. Death is natural, after all.

Liberators ask whether these people would adopt the same attitude if someone was coming after their five year old brother to slaughter and eat him? Would they allow him to be murdered if it was assured that he would feel minimal pain at his moment of death? Or would they say he has a life to live, which nobody has a right to end. If the killers reason that the child has had a good life, would it make his murder more acceptable? Of course not, the liberators exclaim!

Some murderers of animals justify their actions by agreeing that humans are animals, too, and animals kill one another. Humans are simply living according to the rule of the jungle. They do not explain why, as animals, humans choose to act like parasites and aggressive carnivores, rather than like peaceful herbivores. They also don't explain how, as ruthless beasts killing and exploiting other creatures, humans can be expected to behave humanely and respectfully towards other humans. When challenged for an answer, they reflexively say that humans are not the same as animals. Humans somehow deserve more respect. To liberators, that statement reveals a prejudice, called speciesism, which involves a belief that non-human species are inferior to humans, as racism is a belief that some races are inferior to others.

Treating animals as inferior and having less value than humans is a feature of even some staunch animal rights defenders, liberators believe. As an example, they refer to the words of the self-proclaimed guru of the American animal rights movement, Dr. Tom Regan. In his Case for Animal Rights, Regan states that the life of a dog is less rich and valuable than that of a human. Regan concludes that the death of a dog would be a lesser harm to the dog than the death of a human would be to the human. Liberators feel that, with friends like this, the animals need no enemies.

Humans have no business assessing how much value or quality a dog, or any creature, has in his life. Liberators consider such assessments to be anthropocentric. From their naturocentric ethic, they believe that humans have no business passing judgment on the quality and value of the life of another creature. Further, what relevance does such a judgment make? It makes no difference what we assume to be the value or quality of a neighbor's life when it comes to our respecting his right to live. And it makes no difference whether that neighbor is a dog being, snail being, fly being, human being, bat being, or giraffe being.

Most people have difficulty not putting the interests of humans before other animals. Liberators believe that if people treated animals like loved members of a family, then they would all be vegans (strict vegetarians who use no animal products at all, including milk or eggs), would not drive cars, would participate in society to the least degree possible, and would not be afraid to showing disdain for animal abusers. They would wash their hands of all animal exploitation, and would focus their activities on freeing animals today, rather than trying to convince people to free them tomorrow. Most people, however, are not willing to take these consistent steps. After all, they don't want to be labeled "extremists" by their animal abusing friends.

Liberators hold that **the animals do not need a human education movement. They need an animal liberation movement.** They are engaged in a war with society to defend their family from attack. They believe that they will never win the war, but it is the only way to rescue individual family members from human tyranny.

In defending their position, liberators ask, what would you do if your sister was being raped each day? Would you have a peaceful talk with the rapists, or write your Congressmen, who is also a rapist? Or should you take a gun and blow the bastards' balls off? Liberators know what their sister would want them to do.

For liberators, it's time to save what animals they can, enabling these innocent beings to live their lives as nature, not man, intended. Liberators celebrate their good fortune of being alive at a time when animals can still live in the wild, limited as it is. They feel they can make a difference, and for each animal they save, they feel it's the difference between life and death.

---

2 The use of the word "Game" in this agency's title is testimony to the anthropocentrism

Chapter Three

HOMO DESTRUCTUS

Liberators have given up on humans. For them, the goal of converting humans into more ethical, sensitive beings, capable of respecting the rights of animals to live, is impossible. They have two reasons for coming to this conclusion. The first is that it is not in the nature of most people to respect non-human life. Second, animal abuse is an intrinsic feature of our society. In this chapter I will explain the first reason, and leave the second for the next chapter.

When we think of the way we should be treating animals, we are thinking about ethical principles. Ethics is usually presented by philosophers, who appeal to people's minds with reasoned arguments about how people should behave. However, **liberators believe that an intellectual approach towards changing people's ethical, or moral, beliefs is doomed to failure. This is because ethics really has little to do with the mind.**

All the reasoning in the world will not get through to a person invested in a particular behavior. **The human mind has a tremendous capacity to close itself off from all reasoning, and insulate itself from moral argument.**

People act from their hearts, not their heads. Every salesperson knows this. They sell the feelings that the purchased item will bring. Children know this technique, too. A tearful eyed plea is much more effective than reasoning in getting parents to comply with wishes.

Humans do things which feel good and avoid things which feel bad. They merely use their minds to justify their feelings.

It's no different for ethicists. Philosophers, like everyone else, begin with a feeling of what is right, an intuitive sense of what should be, and then try to develop arguments to justify those original feelings. Non-philosophers in the general public, who care about ethical principles regarding how to behave towards others, are attracted to those philosophical theories and arguments which reflect and confirm what they already feel is right.

Intellectual arguments, then, are not effective in persuading people to treat non-humans with respect, unless the people already feel that non-humans deserve that respect.[3]

Most people don't even respond to intellectual arguments concerning ethics. When asked why they are eating animals, for example, they will say, "I like the taste." When you push them against the wall with words, showing them that they are inconsistent in their treatment of humans and non-humans, that they are merely being speciesists, they will say, "So I'm speciesist! I'm inconsistent! I'll accept that." Even after you show them what is done to animals in factory farms and by slaughter houses, and even after you explain to them that billions of animals are destroyed that way each year, they still continue to eat flesh, perhaps averting their eyes when passing a particularly grotesque butcher shop. Clearly, their behavior is not a matter of ignorance. Yet your words fell on deaf ears. Why?

Arguments don't change people's behaviors. Only changes in feelings can.

As a simple illustration of this truth, liberators use the example of slaughter house workers. It's clear that these workers know what they are doing. Telling them the facts of animal destruction makes no sense. They live those facts. Yet they still slaughter animals. Why do they continue to do it?

Liberators contend that it is because, while they know what they are doing, they don't feel what they are doing.

As a result, liberators hold that it is useless using ethics to "prove" that animals should or shouldn't be respected in their right to live . All one can say is that one **feels it is wrong** to exploit animals, or that one **feels it is acceptable** to use animals for human ends. The rest of the argument is window dressing, mind games to justify that one's feelings are correct.

This is why liberators conclude that we will never free the animals by talking to abusers about ethics.

At the risk of seeming philosophical themselves, liberators have considered the question, "Why do some people respect animals and others don't?" To answer this they know that they must address the deeper question, "What makes a person ever consider the needs of others?"

Liberators believe a person only considers others when it affects that person's feelings, specifically, his or her feelings of pain or pleasure.

If we like someone, it gives us pleasure to be with them. Our behavior towards them is motivated by the pleasure they give us. On the other hand, we will be motivated to avoid a person who gives us pain.

So long as someone can please or harm us, so long as he affects our lives, we will consider how we treat him.

If pain and pleasure are both motivations, it could be asked which is the stronger. Liberators point out that the work of moral development theorists like Maslow, Erikson, and others, suggest that people must first achieve a level of safety and have basic needs met before higher levels of personal fulfillment and happiness can be attained. This means that people need to have their stomachs full and have warmth and shelter as prerequisites for a happy life. Without these basic requirements being met, people will feel pain and its associated feeling, fear. Consumed by pain and fear, people cannot truly develop into happy, fulfilled human beings.

Also, pain and fear can cause a highly morally developed person to act on the lowest level of selfish, basic need fulfillment. The most generous, compassionate, friendly person can turn into a murderous beast under the right conditions of fear and pain. **This, liberators conclude, is because pain is a greater motivation than pleasure on a basic, fundamental level.**

They say that personal reflection supports this point. The example they use is that you cannot enjoy very much when you have a headache. **The pain overwhelms the pleasure.** Also, when you are sick and in pain your consideration of others melts away, revealing a basic self-interest in getting yourself better. This makes good biological sense. Pain tells the organism that he or she is in danger of being damaged, with the ultimate threat of death. Pleasure becomes a luxury that an organism cannot afford until its basic survival needs are again satisfied.

Liberators, therefore, believe that **pain is more powerful than pleasure in motivating people. Fear is a component of pain, and is an extremely efficient means of controlling people's behaviors.** Fear is a form of emotional pain. Unlike physical pain, fear can motivate people without being accompanied by physical contact. And fear is used all the time to keep humans under control.

For example, the fear of going to jail keeps many people from disobeying laws. Peer groups control members through the fear of rejection. The Internal Revenue Service controls taxpayers through the fear of an audit. Advertisers try to create a need for a product in the minds of consumers, and use fear when they suggest that people will suffer without fulfilling that need.

Of course, **sometimes people are pushed in opposite directions by their fears.** For example, someone may believe that eating meat is unhealthy, and wishes to avoid meat for fear of getting ill. On the other hand, that person may fear losing her meat eating spouse by seeming too different and extreme. For that person, it comes down to which fear is greater.

All those interested in influencing people's behaviors use fear as a manipulation tool. Exploiting this observation of human nature,

liberators feel that changing people's behaviors requires that the fear, and, hence, the pain, of doing the undesirable activity must become greater than the pain and fear of not doing it.

In terms of stopping animal abuse, liberators feel it makes more sense to have people fear what will happen to them if they continue to abuse animals, than to debate with them over the ethical ramifications of their actions.

To liberators, then, fear and pain are the primary motivations of people. Moving on to the weaker, but real, motivating force of pleasure, it is clear that people get pleasure from those they like, and treat them differently from those they dislike. What makes people like or dislike others?

Liberators believe it is our ability to identify with others, which is another way of saying our ability to empathize with them, that determines whether we will like them or dislike them.

Empathy is a feeling we get when we believe we can feel what another is feeling. It has nothing to do with the mind, but with the heart, and is therefore real and powerful in its effect on our behavior. It is the way we see our connection to others, and identify with their reality.

Without empathy we cannot feel affection for others. It is the basis of friendship and love. It feels good. And we need it.

According to liberators, love, the most pleasant form of empathy, is the second greatest motivator of humans, second only to pain and fear.

Liberators say that the reason we need love and empathy is because we all feel alone in the world. Humans are an alienated species, unsure of their connection with the rest of nature. It's a frightening world when you have no real clue how to act, no internal instincts telling you what is healthy or harmful. If we had such knowledge, we wouldn't need ethics or religion to tell us how to live. Both try to address human behavior and our place in the world. Ever since there have been people, there have been religious and moral codes trying to make sense out of the chaos of the human condition. This basic human existential uncertainty makes people lonely and frightened. Friendship is welcome relief.

On the other side of this existential coin is the need to feel control in the world. Liberators believe that power and control issues dominate most people's lives. If people can't be in control over their own lives, then they will try to be in control over the lives of others.

People fear being out of control, because being out of control is painful. We try to feel we will be okay in the world, that the environment is not hostile, and that our needs will be met. Seeking control over others is one way humans achieve an illusory peace in their minds that the world is a safe, manageable place.

Love for others and power over others are mutually exclusive. You cannot love someone you exploit, or exploit someone you love.

The way most people handle this paradox is by loving some and controlling others. And since control is often exploitative, it requires that you feel little or no empathy for those controlled, so you can avoid suffering along with them as you exploit them.

To illustrate this point, liberators use the example of Nazi doctors who conducted heinous experiments on Jews during the day, while acting as loving husbands and fathers at night. Humans label a group as "other," using race, nationality, sex, or species as the basis for the distinction, and consider that group unworthy of empathy and, therefore, a reasonable target for exploitation. So long as humans have some other group with whom they can identify and find empathy and love, they can satisfy their need for affection. By splitting groups this way, people allow themselves the pleasure of love with some groups, and the reduction of pain through the exploitation of other groups.

The groups they are kind to consist of human beings, particularly those of equal or greater power. The ones exploited are typically powerless, unable to reciprocate aggression, which is the case with non-human beings.

This is an important point about the liberators' beliefs that deserves emphasis. The conflict between fear and pleasure, control and empathy, plays out in the following way. If you have power over others, then you will not fear them. This means you can treat them any way you like, whether it be exploitatively or fairly, and they will simply have to accept it. If treated exploitatively, then they have no recourse but to suffer. If treated fairly, then they have the choice of reciprocating your fairness. Most likely, since you have more power, they will always treat you fairly, or even give you more than you deserve, which is a form of self-exploitation, regardless of your treatment of them. In short, you have all the power and you call the shots.

On the other hand, if the others have equal or greater power than you have, the tables are turned. Your treatment of them is tempered by the constant awareness that they can reciprocate kindness or aggression, and you may lose if it is aggression. Fear of reprisals keeps you in check. Of course, if you like the more powerful individuals and wish to treat them fairly, all the better. But you would not treat them in anything but a fair manner, and you may even chose to exploit yourself and give them more than they deserve as an insurance policy to soothe your fears.

What this boils down to is that those in power have the option of treating others as they wish, with no fear that the others might reciprocate evil for evil. Those out of power are moved by fear to comply with the wishes of the powerful. Another way of saying this is that **humans interact with one another according to a pecking order. What this means is that treating others with liberty, fraternity and equality are not natural human tendencies. For most people, it's a peck or be pecked world.**

When people chose groups to exploit, the least powerful are the easiest target. Non-human animals have no power by themselves to respond to human aggression and exploitation. **Animals are helpless to suffer the fate of human power over their lives.**

Because humans consider animals to be objects undeserving of empathy, they do not recognize the pain they are causing them. They have disqualified animals as feeling beings capable of suffering and having interests of their own. These people are, therefore, numb to their cries and pain. This numbness allows abusers to sleep at night, and kill during the day.4

Liberators believe that people consider the needs of others only when it affects their pleasure or pain. Those with empathy for animals respect the animals. They get pleasure identifying with non-human beings, and enjoy seeing them free. People such as liberators respect all beings as equal members of the family of life, entitled to their moment on the planet. Instead of seeing animals as objects of control, they see them as objects of love. Liberators satisfy their need for control by focusing on their own lives, and committing themselves to a lifestyle consistent with a respect for all creatures.

Why do some people develop empathy for animals while others don't? Liberators believe it depends on who they are, what their life experiences have been, how open their hearts are, and how seduced they are by cruel social institutions. What makes some people racist or sexist? The same forces are at work in our dealings with animals.

To liberators this means that, if you don't have empathy for animals, at least to some degree, then you will not understand any argument for respecting their autonomy. Further, animals are helpless and easy prey for human control, since they can't fight back.

Liberators believe these two factors are major obstacles to changing people's behaviors towards animals. The impact of these obstacles has made human history a non-stop legacy of animal abuse and exploitation. **Human brutality to animals, and even to humans who can't fight back, has been a fact of life since the beginning of recorded time. It is clear to liberators that the obstacles to humans developing a sensitivity to animals are insurmountable.**

The lesson liberators draw from their study of human nature is that the only way to stop oppression of animals is by creating a fear of reprisals for such acts. Animals cannot do this by themselves, but need liberators to act as their agents.

In other words, they believe that reasoning will not help, since people are motivated by their hearts, not minds, to oppress others. Reprisals are the only effective means. The fear and pain of reprisals can offset the existential fear that control over the animals was meant to satisfy. Only when the weak become strong will exploitative humans mind their manners.

Either animals will be respected because people love them, or they will be respected because people are afraid of what will happen to them if they don't treat them with respect. That is the rule liberators use for understanding how humans deal with others. Since animals can't retaliate against human aggression and exploitation by themselves, it is up to liberator agents to do so for them.

Let me deal with some objections to the liberator argument. One objection may be that many people can "love" animals, yet still be willing, and eager, to kill them for food. For example, I know a farmer who raises pigs, and "loves" the piglets all the way to the butcher shop. She also gets calves as pets for two years, and then "puts them in the freezer." Can't people "love" animals and exploit them at the same time?

Of course not, say the liberators! **What these abusive humans feel foranimals is not love.** People are motivated by self interest as they try to maximize pleasure and minimize pain. If letting a pig grow is pleasurable, then the pig will survive. But once eating the pig gives someone more pleasure than letting it live, watch out pig.

This question also raises an important point about empathy. **Liberators feel that many so called "animal lovers" are not actually identifying and empathizing with animals, but are merely projecting onto animals their own beliefs about what the animals should be feeling.**

I have a personal experience to illustrate the liberators' point. Some horse "lovers" were sad that a horse was being underfed by some irresponsible people, and were angry that the police were refusing to do anything about it. They seemed to be people sensitive to horses' needs. Yet they surprised me when I asked: "How do you feel about the carriage horses that are worked up and down this street giving rides to tourists?"

They did not go into a tirade, explaining that such treatment of horses is slavery and an abomination. Instead, they responded: "Those horses are cared for. They are fed well and nicely groomed. And they're work horses. I don't think they would be happy if they couldn't work."

Liberators would interpret this as an illustration of how humans can fool themselves into thinking that they are feeling empathy, when all they are really doing is projecting onto others their own feelings and assumptions of how the other should be feeling.

How many times have you felt intense emotions after some stirring event, and someone tells you, quite erroneously, that he knows exactly how you feel? That's projection. It's dealing with others in one's own reality, instead of trying to get into their reality. Most people haven't the slightest clue how others feel. They use their minds and assume that they know who you are and how you should be reacting to certain situations.

But empathy is not a mind trip. It is a way of communicating that takes place without words. It is intuitive. For a society that underrates intuition and overrates intellect, liberators feel it is no surprise that people have not developed their empathic skills.

This is why someone can love pigs and still say that it's all right to kill them for their flesh. If they feel it's all right, and project that feeling onto the pigs, then they can feel that the pigs somehow feel it's all right, too. Further supporting this illusion is the inability of the pigs to answer back verbally, explaining that the feeling attributed to them was mistaken.

Liberators believe that true empathy with others is difficult. It takes patience, a quiet mind, and a willingness to see reality differently, as others see it. This task is difficult enough with other humans. We are reminded how little we understand others whenever we come into contact with another culture. Suddenly, our assumptions about behaviors don't work. But dealing with other human cultures is easy when compared to dealing with non-human cultures. The behaviors of mice beings, bat beings, and mink beings are truly foreign to human beings.

Liberators assert that seeing the world as a non-human being sees it requires that we leave our anthropocentric way of regarding other

beings and things, and develop a naturocentric perspective. Such a view would place common features among animals as a foundation for understanding, and thereby empathizing, with them. We may not understand the behaviors of all other creatures, but we do know that they are living on the same planet as we are, and have the same physical reality as we have.

The more we see ourselves as animals, connected with other creatures, as well as with plants, streams, rocks, clouds, and all of nature, the greater our effectiveness in truly gaining insight into the feelings of our brothers and sisters.

Liberators think that this is a tall order for most people to fill. **Liberators believe that most people live in their own worlds, and don't even know how to relate to other humans.** This is all a function of their alienation from nature, including their own natures as human animals. The more alienated people are, the less they can identify with others, be they human or non-human. That is because identification requires self-understanding. In common parlance, you must understand yourself before you can understand others.

To make human empathy with non-humans even more improbable, people are told how different they are from other animals. We have souls, animals don't. We have thoughts and feelings, animals don't. We are made in God's image. We have dominion over other animals. We are the chosen creatures.

Even the distinction human/animal, which is institutionalized in the "animal" rights movement, implies that we are different from non-humans. In effect, humans see themselves as non-animals. How can anyone develop empathy with others who are by definition different? Liberators claim it's impossible.

Liberators believe empathy is needed for moral behavior. The obstacles to developing true empathy make moral behavior towards non-human beings difficult for even conscientious individuals, not to mention for disinterested people.

Another objection might arise at this point. If liberators say that self-alienation is at the root of human cruelty, perhaps animal lovers should address human pain with the hope of somehow "healing" humankind? The result of people being healed might eventually trickle down to help oppressed animals. Another way some people put this is that we can't help the animals until we first address human needs.

Liberators say that there are two false assumptions used for this objection.

One is that people are basically good. The ridiculousness of this notion will be addressed in the "Myth of Non-Violence" chapter. The second assumption is that such healing of human nature is possible, usually through education, reasoned debate, unconditional love, and patience. We have already discussed this fallacy.

To liberators, this approach is anthropocentrism in disguise. Attempting to "heal" humans to save nonhumans is useless.

First, liberators consider that the pain which causes the need for control arises from a deep human existential crisis, something that has not been solved since recorded history. Humans have never felt at home on this planet. Our alienation is almost definitional of what it means to be human. We just don't have the answers to this existential question, and we never will. That is the cause of our eternal anxiety, and our desire for control. It is not about to go away by debate and education.

Second, **taking the time to try and "heal" humankind is a luxury animals cannot afford. They are suffering today, even as you read this, not in the thousands, but in the millions and millions. If liberators truly wish to help animals defend themselves, they believe they must do what the animals need right now. And to the liberators, that means liberation, not counseling and unconditional love for their oppressors.**

You may still not understand the liberators view of the use of militant tactics to stop animal oppressors. Let me explain their position with an example that they like to use. People believe that the use of force, even deadly force, is acceptable when being attacked, as a form of self-defense. People also expect an innocent bystander to assist a victim of assault if that victim is in need of help, even if that assistance must be the use of deadly force. In both of these cases, people allow the use of force on the basis of self-defense, whether the force was executed by oneself or by the agent of the victim. Liberators believe they are simply using force in self-defense as agents for animal victims of human oppression.

To the liberators, the animals are being brutalized. They are helpless. Liberators feel that they have every moral right to defend them. And they believe humans will not stop abusing non-humans without militant intervention.

Some readers may disagree with the liberators, and insist that dialogue with abusers is potentially valuable. In response to this, liberators point out that, even if people were persuaded by ideas instead of force, the fact is that most people care nothing about moral issues. Fighting with words instead of force is a waste of time. People who hope to use words to change abusers do not like to think that their efforts have been useless. But look at the evidence.

The Meyers/Briggs Test is a personality profile test, well recognized, respected and used by psychologists. It has helped psychologists determine that the general population of this country falls into the following approximate personality categories:

– 38% of the people are action oriented, deeply committed to an activity while they are doing it. They seek the "gusto" in life. They live in the present, and tend to have physical occupations. Intense, active involvement is important to them.

– 12% are interested in their intellectual competence. They usually get jobs in the sciences. Ideas and rigorous thinking are important to them.

– 38% are duty and responsibility focused. They are concerned with their place in the society, they respect laws and authority and they are loyal to the system. Accountants, bankers and administrators fit into this category. Maintaining the status quo is important to them.

– 12% are concerned with self-actualization and spirituality, and question the significance of life and their place in the world. Ethical issues and interpersonal relations are important to them.

Naturally, nobody is purely one category or another. Overlap does occur. But in general, **there is only a small section of the public, about 12%, that even cares about the animal issues raised in this book.** Of course, 12% of the 270 million people in this country amounts to about 30 million people, which is a significant number. That some of these people are awakening to the fact of animal abuse has given the animal movement a great surge of growth and support. It has been estimated that 10 million people are members of animal organizations. When you consider that these issues were a rarity only a decade ago, the momentum of the movement seems great, indeed.

Liberators believe that as a result of these newly interested people in the movement, certain businesses have become willing to change their ways. Vegetarian food is more available than before (although most alleged vegetarian items have milk products or eggs). Some cosmetic companies have decided to stop animal testing on their premises. And even newspaper, magazine, television and radio coverage of animal issues has increased, reflecting a rise in awareness. Changes have certainly been made as a result of efforts to influence and educate this 12% of the population.

Such changes, however, are more window dressing than substance, according to the liberators. Restaurants, cosmetic companies and the media will adapt to consumer demand. If there is a profit in catering to the interests of animal lovers, then some businesses will rush to fill that niche.

Before we give the non-violent approach more credit than it deserves, liberators ask that we reflect on some actual changes. Vegetarianism has become increasingly popular, although still to a very small segment of the population, primarily because of its apparent health benefits to humans. In other words, they are vegetarian for anthropocentric and egocentric reasons.

So long as people change their behaviors for personal gain, rather than for ethical reasons, there is always the possibility that they will change again, listening to the next salesman of health and beauty. The meat and medical industries know this. Liberators feel that is why these industries are fighting back to maintain animal abuse. They use the message that lean meat is good and essential for health. They know that health minded people will eat flesh again if told it is good for them.

And they are successful in pushing their message. Witness how many "vegetarian" people revert to a meat based diet for fear of protein or calcium deficiency. Most vegetarians strike a bargain, hoping to get the best of both camps' advice, by eating dairy products and eggs. Is this really a victory for the animal movement, liberators ask?

As another example, consider the cruelty free shoe market. Stores like Payless Shoe Stores offer plastic and canvas shoes. Non-violent animal lovers are quick to claim this as a success of their approach. But, liberators ask, how many people in the movement still wear leather and put fashion before ethics? Is the success of stores like Payless due to the support of animal lovers shunning leather? Or is it that plastic and canvas shoes are cheaper than leather ones? Liberators feel people today are attracted to low cost merchandise. Payless and others stores like it appeal to budget minded people. That's why it's called "Payless" and not "Cruelless". Does that qualify the stores' increased popularity as a victory for the animals, liberators wonder?

On the other hand, liberators state, little has changed in the area of animal research. If anything, things have gotten worse. The creation of genetic engineering techniques have opened up new avenues for animal exploitation. Strains of mice can now be produced, **and are being patented** with certain genetic derangements. The biomedical carnage against animals has continued unabated, except for some increased paperwork that vivisectors must complete. Liberators point out that, despite the growing awareness of such abuses, however, animal lovers still flock to physicians who are trained by bloodthirsty vivisectors, and buy drugs which were tested on animals.

Another failure of non-violent movement raised by liberators is the hunting situation. According to liberators, virtually nothing significant for animals has been achieved over the past decade when it comes to hunting. In fact, there are now hunter harassment laws preventing animal supporters from going into the woods and interfering with the killing.

Why have vivisection and hunting been resistant to progress, while other areas have been more flexible to change? To liberators, the answer is simple. Consumers have an effect on the balance sheet of consumer oriented companies, like restaurants and cosmetic manufacturers. It is no skin off of their noses to add a cruelty free item to their list of products, as when Burger King sells vegeburgers along with its Whoppers.

However, the drug and medical industries know that people will consume their products regardless of animal testing. As discussed above, when people are in pain, their morals often go out the window. As for hunting, that is an isolated business, unaffected by the common person's interests and biases. Hunters buy guns and ammunition from specialty shops, and pay licensing fees to support government agencies overseeing their hunting grounds. The general public has little impact on their activities.

In short, liberators ask that animal lovers be realistic in assessing the successes of the non-violence approach in making a difference for the animals. True, some changes have been made. But liberators insist that people assess those changes in the context of other societal influences, such as the economy, and consider the fickle interests of self-centered consumers whose main concern is personal health and longevity.

According to liberators, all changes that have been made for the animals have been a direct result of an appeal to human self-interest. The popularity of vegetarianism is one example of this fact.

Many groups fighting animal research tell the public that such research is bad for human health. Stop vivisection because it kills humans! Hans Reusch's approach is purely of this type, as he exposes the various ways in which people have been killed by animal research.

Legislative initiatives against trapping have to appeal to the risk of animal traps to innocent children or people's pets, rather than to the wildlife they are intended to kill!

Attempts to stop pound seizures, in which pound animals are sold to research labs, have to address whether or not using those animals in research can help improve human health. As a result, those trying to stop pound seizures argue that animals from pounds have poor health and uncertain medical backgrounds, making them unsuitable for any scientifically valid, reproducible study. Groups like the Medical Research Modernization Committee specifically attack animal research for its ineffectiveness in **helping humans**.

The cosmetic industry seems at first glance to be an exception to this requirement that the animal movement appeal to self-interest to get changes. Actually, it is no exception at all. Cosmetic products are sold for the feelings and images they create for their users. To fight against animal testing, pictures of blinded rabbits and other animal abuses are shown to consumers, associating cruelty with certain cosmetic products. On the other hand, pictures of gentle, beautiful people caressing warm, fuzzy animals are used to associate kindness and compassion with products not tested on animals. Consumer self-interest in looking beautiful motivates some people to buy products unassociated with animal cruelty, since animal cruelty is clearly not beautiful. **To liberators, this need for animal groups to appeal to human self-interest means that these groups are really working on a human-centered movement, rather than an animal movement.** Any gains for the animals comes as a fortunate outcome of the process.

The most positive statement which liberators feel can be made about the non-violent approach is that it can educate some people in the 12% of the public who are interested in moral issues. Some of these people will constitute a new market for animal-friendly consumer goods and services. But in the broader picture, this is a drop in the bucket, and there is no good reason to believe that the trend is irreversible.

To liberators, the sad fact is that not many people want to help the animals. Most people are happy enough getting through the day in one piece. They don't have the energy, or inclination, to address social or moral issues. They constitute the majority of humans in this country, and probably in the world. Liberators know the saints were always fewer than the sinners.

What this means is that moral arguments coming from proponents of various, opposing positions are competing for the attention of that small 12% of society who care about such issues. Working with this target audience to generate behavioral changes is not easy.

Liberators recognize that people hate to change. Humans are habit forming creatures. Someone can see *The Animals Film,* with its graphic display of animal slaughter, agree that the scenes are disgusting, and still eagerly devour a veal cutlet or piece of fried chicken. "I've eaten meat all my life," they rationalize.

Psychologists explain that people have a narrow tolerance for change. If they are pushed too far, exceeding that tolerance, they rebel and go in the opposite direction. This is why some activists believe that we must change people slowly, allowing their tolerance limits to adjust as they move along in the right direction.

Forces tear at people in every direction trying to manipulate them. Animal abusers outnumber people concerned about animals by 100:1, and can just as easily outspend their opposition in advertising and propaganda. People will ultimately be pulled away from supporting animals, as humans are brainwashed by Madison Avenue executives.

Also, **people have to be willing to change**. Animal abuse is a large part of everyone's life in this society, as the next chapter will discuss. The inertia against change is tremendous.

Finally, even if we could get people to change a little in their behaviors, there must be some way of reinforcing that change to prevent people from having a relapse of old behaviors. Many people say they used to be vegetarian, or even vegan, but lost interest, or got into a relationship with a meat eater, causing them to return to flesh as food. Liberators believe that, with society entrenched in animal abuse, making a cruelty free lifestyle an effort to maintain, such behavior reinforcement for respectful treatment of animals is not forthcoming.

Liberators know that people, even the 12% of society interested in moral issues, are weak, stubborn, frightened, irrational, habitual, spiteful, inconsistent, angry, vicious creatures. Dialogue may or may not have any effect on reaching the 12% of the population; but it is certainly a waste of time for the other 88%. We may be able to battle with words for the 12%; but the animals need liberators to battle with force to influence the other 88%.

Liberators ask that animal lovers be realistic and consider what must be done to save animals. They ask what you would do if your sister or brother was imprisoned in a torture chamber, soon to be executed. Would you talk to the prison guards and torturer about human rights? Would you write your Congressman? Hell, no, they exclaim! You'd be doing everything in your power to rescue your family member. To liberators, talk is cheap, and when it comes to ethics, they feel talk is bullshit!

They believe the animals are helpless without them. It is up to human beings to defend them, to truly act as their agents. Speaking on the animals' behalf will not suffice – it hasn't helped oppressed human groups to just speak about their freedom. **Liberators feel we must act for the animals. We must do for them what we believe they would do for themselves.**

And what do liberators believe the animals would do? They would escape from their captors. They would shoot back when shot at. They would destroy the cages that confined them, so they could not be used again. They would damage roads that made way for the destructive force of automobiles. They would burn down research facilities, and kill animal researchers, who daily destroy their kin for profit and amusement. **They would form an underground of saboteurs to disrupt the machinery of the vast human killing machine called society.**

If people had the courage to live up to their commitment to be agents for the animals, then they would do all the above, say the liberators. Indeed, liberators are already doing it! If it is hopeless to try changing people, perhaps we can change society? What do the liberators say about that? Let's talk about that issue next.

---

3 Liberators recognize that there are exceptions to this rule. Some people change their feelings regarding animals as a result of education concerning the forms and pervasiveness of animal abuse. Such transformations are rare, however, and are only possible for a small percentage of the population, as discussed later in this chapter.

4 The inability of some people to relate to animals is made clear when they ask: "Don't plants have rights, too?" All animal activists have heard that question. Liberators believe such a question is never asked by someone who is truly concerned about plants, or animals. The point of the question is to show that animal defenders are inconsistent in drawing a line between animals and vegetables. The questioners assume that there is no morally relevant difference between asparagus and giraffes, so that killing asparagus is morally equivalent to killing giraffes. Naturally, the questioners have no doubt that humans are different in a morally significant way from both animals and vegetables, and, therefore, deserve special consideration. In actuality, then, their question reflects their own bias in considering animals to be the same as vegetables. This is evidence of their deep alienation from animals. Such people have no hope of identifying with animals, just as they can never identify with plants (unless they themselves are vegetables!)

Chapter Four

THE EVERYDAY HOLOCAUST

Liberators believe that today, more than at any other time in history, people are a product of society. Our lives are filled with messages from advertisers telling us how to act, think and feel. Whether it's television, radio, billboards, newspapers, magazines, books, or the mail, people are under constant bombardment from advertisers trying to brainwash consumers. And it works. Advertisers were even able to get people to twice elect a mindless actor to the office of President of the United States!

In a world where your senses are overloaded with bullshit, all of which concerns people, it's hard to think about animals. Americans think of themselves as the freest people on Earth, but they are controlled and manipulated like cartoon characters, living a fantasy existence designed by Madison Avenue animators. **Even if human nature was amenable to an ethic of respect for animal life, this society would not allow it, say the liberators.**

People who believe that animals have a right to live their own lives free from human exploitation have been called "terrorists" by key figures in the animal abuse status quo, such as Dr. Louis Sullivan, Secretary of the U.S Department of Health and Human Services. Fearing that such comments will alienate the general populace and cause a loss of public sympathy, animal supporters condemn all illegal animal liberation tactics and promise to work within the system, just as the abusers want them to. They blame all the "terrorist" activities on the A.L.F., which they promise has nothing to do with themselves, and pledge allegiance to the rules and laws of society.

What these animal supporters don't realize, according to the liberators, is that the abusers are correct. **If we were true supporters of animals, we would be terrorists.** The abusers see that **the logical, consistent extension of an animal rights philosophy is not only the liberation of animals from all forms of abuse, but the destruction of the abusive society. According to liberators, nothing short of a complete revolution will gain animal freedom.**

Liberators expect that this statement is more difficult for animal supporters to accept than it is for animal abusers. This is because people who wish to defend the rights of animals are still, for the most part, invested in remaining members of this society. They do not like to think that living in society as a normal citizen and defending animals against human tyranny are mutually exclusive. But, according to liberators, they are! **Liberators believe it is impossible to be a true animal rights supporter and still be a member of this society. This is because animal abuse is an integral feature of this system.**

Liberators explain their view using the following argument.

Animal abuse in society takes two forms – overt and covert. The overt forms are common knowledge to anyone who has read a book on animal rights or has seen a movie describing animal exploitation. Any readers not aware of this information can refer to Peter Singer's Animal Liberation. Information can also be obtained from national organizations like People for the Ethical Treatment of Animals (P.E.T.A.). Or call your local animal rights group.

Overt forms of animal exploitation are a part of our society's daily consumerism. Most obvious is the use of non-humans for food. This is by far the largest and most hideous crime against our non-human family. Each year in this country alone, 5.5 **billion** chickens, 40 **million** cows, and 95 **million** pigs are murdered. That's in addition to **millions** of sheep, turkeys, ducks and geese killed. Nobody even counts the **billions** of fish, shrimp, clams, oysters and other "seafood" animals people eat, not to mention the **billions** of "trash fish," sea turtles and marine mammals and other non-target animals destroyed in the hunting process.

Another overt abuse of animals is the use of their body parts for **clothing and ornamentation**. Perhaps the most common body part used for these purposes is skin. The appeal of fur leads to the worldwide brutal massacre of over 90 million animal beings each year, including coyote beings, wolf beings, fox beings, mink beings, rabbit beings, bobcat beings, lynx beings, muskrat beings, squirrel beings, raccoon beings, beaver beings, skunk beings and any other animal beings who are unfortunate enough to have been born with a beautiful coat that humans wish to steal. Approximately half of these beings, mostly foxes and minks, are "farmed" under appalling conditions. The other half is trapped out of their homes in the wild.

Leather is more than a by-product of the meat industry. It is a significant profit maker. Since so many cow beings are slaughtered each year, there is lots of cow skin available for inclusion in products from shoes and other clothing, to handbags, steering wheel covers and furniture upholstery. The reason it is so difficult for vegans to find cruelty-free products, that is, items without any dead animal ingredients, is that the slaughter industry has so successfully marketed its products.

Feathers of slaughtered birds make the down of sleeping bags and the stuffing of pillows. Seashells serve as ornamentation, with their purchasers rarely considering that these perfect shells did not wash ashore, and were not uninhabited. Silk is obtained from industrious silkworm beings, who are boiled alive to remove the product of their labor.

Even living animals serve as ornamentation. Fish tanks and bird cages are a private zoo for the common man, displaying animals as if they were merely pretty or amusing objects, never really meant to live free. Domestic dog and cat beings are often treated as nothing more than exotic furniture. And in the streets of tourist towns, horse beings with blinders, a mouth bit, and a yoke, are treated as slaves and forced to pull carriages loaded with insensitive people, who do not see beyond the horses' braided manes to notice the boredom and fatigue in their eyes.

Sports enthusiasts use animals in overtly abusive ways, as well. Some get pleasure entering the homes of wild animals, the forest, desert, lakes, etcetera, and killing them with either bullets or arrows. Others enjoy shooting animals released from cages, as in the Hegins, Pennsylvania annual dove being shoot. Sports fishermen get great pleasure hunting for sea creatures, delighting in the "play" of the animals who try to escape from the pain in their mouths or, if they swallowed the hook, in their stomachs. And some rough and tough cowboys get pleasure beating up farm animals in rodeos, the American equivalent of the bullfight.

The use of animals in **testing cosmetics** is an abuse animal supporters are trying to make overt. Some people now realize that their household cleansers, cosmetics, perfumes, and soaps were developed with animal testing. Animals are poisoned in the LD (Lethal Dosage) 50 test, wherein enough of the product is force fed to the animals to kill 50% of the test population. Rabbits are blinded by the Draize test as a product is forcefully applied to their eyes. Besides killing through these tests, the products themselves contain ingredients derived from dead animals. Soaps are often made from animal fat, another application of dead animal products obtained from slaughter houses.

Both over the counter and prescription **drugs** are developed and tested on animals. The drug industry is a multi-billion dollar enterprise, and tens of millions of animals are killed each year to develop new agents. The **biomedical research** industry is intimately associated with the drug world, and kills 100 million animals each year. Not all of these drugs are for direct human consumption. One half of all antibiotics produced are fed to animals destined for slaughter, to minimize the deleterious effects of factory farming on their growth and development. Human beings, of course, consume these drugs indirectly, as they consume the animals' flesh.

Movie makers use non-human beings in their productions. As in circuses, these animals are taught to perform tricks to amuse insensitive humans. The glitter of Hollywood blinds people to the abuses that occur backstage, where the animals are trained not to be animals, but puppets.

These are just some of the overt abuses to animals. They are overt because they are easy to see by the unprejudiced eye. Before getting to the covert forms, however, liberators always like to emphasize one heinous abuse of animals which even many alleged vegetarians support. It is the use of animals in the production of dairy products and eggs. Many people think of these forms of liquid flesh as benign, since the animal is not killed in the process. What could be more natural and peaceful than a cup of yogurt?

Few people know about the connection between the dairy industry and the veal production business. The same people who shun veal should never drink milk.

A cow being is impregnated to produce calves and begin lactating. The calves are removed from their mother within days of birth and sent to veal producers, where they are chained by the neck in crates to minimize their movement and prevent them from even turning around. This torture is intended to make their flesh tender, since unused muscle has smaller, more easily chewable fibers. They spend the next few months of their lives chained this way in darkness, drinking powdered milk laced with antibiotics, and suffering from pneumonia and diarrhea, until the time of their slaughter ends their pain. They will soon be replaced, since their mother will again be impregnated to keep her milk and veal production up. She will no longer be used as a veal and milk production machine, however, once she is incapable of producing profitable quantities of milk. At that time she is slaughtered and sent to the pet food producers.

Eggs also seem cruelty free. But once you reflect on the horrendous conditions of factory farm laying chicken beings, and the fate of all chickens, even "free-range" ones, once they do not produce enough to support their feed bill, it is clear to liberators that they do not want these family members to be treated the way they are.

According to this liberator argument, no product coming from domesticated animals can ever be cruelty free. Domestication is slavery in service to humans. Through genetic manipulation people have selected character traits for animals to perform specific functions. Today's chickens lay unnaturally high numbers of eggs. Cows produce so much milk their udders are virtually hanging on the ground, and are kicked each time the animal walks. These freaks are products of mankind's ingenuity and exploitative propensity. Nothing from them is ever cruelty free.

You might agree that the above abuses of non-humans must end. Towards that goal you commit yourself to a strict vegan diet and lifestyle, avoiding all animal products and animal suffering in your food, clothing and household goods. You will watch no movies which exploit animals, and avoid zoos and circuses. And so long as you don't engage in abusive sports, you can live a fairly peaceful life, and feel you are a true animal supporter.

Unfortunately, according to liberators, you would be fooling yourself!

Covert animal abuse is a normal, virtually unavoidable part of our society. This nation was built by people who ignored the rights of any beings other than white, Christian Europeans. We all know what happened to the American Indians. But they were treated like kings compared to our non-human family members.

Consider for a moment what it would be like if we had no roads with cars and trucks traveling along them. The image is impossible to envision, unless you imagine some tribal existence where small bands of people live in harmony with nature. In the reality of today's cities and interstate commerce, the image is pure fantasy. But did you know that road kills are the number two destroyers of non-human life? **One million animals are run over by cars and trucks each day in the United States alone!**

Liberators want you to think about that the next time you drive. If you are going to a rally to protest against fur, you may accidentally hit a squirrel being, or skunk being, or raccoon being, or deer being. And the situation is even more devastating if you consider insect beings. Some people extend their compassion even to spider beings, fly beings, moth beings, and other small beings. They would let them out of their homes if caught inside. And many vegans avoid honey and silk because of respect for the bees and worms, who clearly make their products for their own use, not man's. Yet these same conscientious people slaughter these creatures, sometimes in the hundreds, when they drive just a few miles in their metal assassins.

If you really loved animals, you would not drive your car. You may think that suggestion sounds absurd. But the fact is that you are driving through the homes of other creatures when we take a ride through the forest, desert, countryside, or even the city streets. Animals do not see the highway as off-limits. They cannot understand the concept of road easements. The road is simply a cleared area of their living space. They are sometimes even attracted to the asphalt pavement for reasons of warmth, or to scavenge the decaying flesh of other creatures who were flattened and splattered by some vehicle. Driving a car is like entering a crowded forest and shooting a gun. At some point you are bound to hit and kill someone.

If you have not killed any mammals or birds while driving, it's only a matter of time. Of course, we call such events "accidents" when they occur. That means we didn't plan on them happening. If you fired a gun in the woods, say, while target shooting, and some innocent animal was shot and killed, you would call that an accident, too. But knowing that someone could have been shot by your target practice makes that act irresponsible. You certainly would not practice shooting in an area where children were playing. If you tried you would be arrested. And if you killed someone, you would be charged with manslaughter. The fact that it was an accident when a child was shot does not release you from the burden of having killed him.

According to the liberators, the same thing goes for driving a car through other creatures' back yards. Some will die because of your actions, and you know that. To continue to drive despite this fact is irresponsible and an act of aggression against these innocent creatures.

Liberators explain that it doesn't matter, from the animals' point of view, what your intentions were. You may have been driving to the pound to rescue a dog. The animals you kill will not rest more peacefully knowing that you meant them no harm.

People don't want to think about this problem. Even those who are conscientious about their respect for animals ignore this issue. Those who have mentioned it lament that little is done about road kills, and suggest that people drive carefully. What a bullshit suggestion, exclaim the liberators! Would you accept people driving carefully through your backyard with your five year old brothers and sisters running around, the liberators ask?

The fact that this is such a difficult issue is precisely because driving is an integral feature of modern day life. People drive to work, shopping centers, schools, friends and family, entertainment centers, health care providers, and vacation spots. The car has become a necessity of life, a fact that pleases every auto manufacturer, oil driller, highway constructor, steel plant operator, and tire maker.

Not only do individual families believe they need cars to get around, but our food, fuel, clothing, and nearly every other consumer item are shipped by truck. The nation's, and world's, communities are not self-sufficient. Transportation is the life blood of the world economy. Without it people would have to live in small, self-reliant bands.

Liberators are all for leveling society and living within a small band of peaceful people. That is a fantasy that has been fulfilled for a few people of like mind and heart who have decided to "drop out" and live on a commune. But liberators feel that that would not solve the greater problem of road kills, since the bulk of our nation's 270 million people are not about to give up their big homes in sprawling cities and suburbs, or their two cars and off road vehicles.

The liberator message is clear: Don't delude yourself. If you participate in this society you are an accessory to this crime against our fellow

creatures. You do not have to run over an animal yourself to be guilty. Guilt is included along with the receipt for every consumer item.

Related to road kills are two other covert abusers. One is the **oil industry**. Most people are now aware of the environmental impact of oil drilling. Their concern, however, is usually directed at the economic impact of oil spills. Will it damage commercial fish hatcheries, or wash up on beaches located in resort areas? Seldom is it considered that the homes of our brothers and sisters are being polluted, regardless of the economic significance of those homes to humans.

Each year there are dozens of oil spills of all sizes, killing millions of animals. Liberators suffer with their brother, the water skimmer, as he flies inches over the water, dipping his lower beak into the top layer of ocean to sieve the water for food, and finds his mouth coated with tar and oil. Liberators can imagine what marine mammals feel when they get covered with oil, the sticky, smelly substance clumping their fur, stinging their eyes, and clogging their nostrils and mouths. It doesn't take much empathy to imagine what these aquatic family members feel when their world is contaminated with oil. And, liberators conclude, it doesn't take a genius to realize that "accidents" will happen, and that more oil spills will occur. Is this enough to stop society from using oil products? Of course not, lament the liberators.

Some people say that they would willingly use an electric powered car, if it was available. Unfortunately, those people regret, it is not available at the present time. If this is your excuse, you should realize what the liberators would say. **If you respected animals, you would not participate in the system of oil production that kills so many creatures.** Also, driving electric cars would still not get you out of animal abuse on the roads.

Even if one ignored these two massive problems in our society, one could not ignore the second covert abuse related to transportation. **Roads** have to be built to allow transportation to occur. The land chosen for their location may already be occupied, and almost assuredly is. If those occupants are human, then the State reimburses them for taking their land. If the occupants are squirrel's, or deer, or woodpeckers, or even millions of insects, there is no consideration made. **Animal beings are treated as natural resources who only receive consideration when they can fulfill a human being's needs. At other times they are mere obstacles, objects that must be cleared out, like dead tree stumps that are uprooted or plowed under, making way for human progress.**

Liberators believe that whenever you drive or consume products of this driving society, you are implicitly accepting the abuse that this transportation system commits against members of our family. Even if you eat a vegetarian diet, consisting of organic food shipped directly from local farms, you are participating in the destructive distribution system that enabled the foods to get to market.

You may be fortunate enough to have missed the deer that ran out of the bushes onto the road a minute before you drove past, or to have swerved in time to not smash the squirrel that darted across the highway just as you approached her foraging area, or to have stopped short in time not to crash into a dog running across the street to catch a cat. **It doesn't matter that you do not have fur sticking to a dent in your front fender. By participating in this cruel system, you have simply let someone else do the killing for you.**

The transportation system is enough of an inherent feature of our society to condemn our system as irrevocably abusive to non-humans. But there's more! **Wildlife habitat destruction** is not only committed in the name of highways. The roads lead to building projects, whether they are new condominiums built on what had been an "undeveloped" hillside, or a strip shopping center constructed on what had been a "vacant" lot consisting of trees and grass.

There are quotation marks around "undeveloped" and "vacant" because these are human-centered words. "Undeveloped" simply means not yet built to human specifications. Trees, moss, and other vegetation, burrows for small animals, ant hills, bee hives, and nests are natural developments in the lives of non-human creatures. Likewise, the notion that an area is "vacant" limits its reference to human inhabitants.

To liberators, the clearing of land is nothing less than theft from its original inhabitants, the animals. People should approach every location on the planet with respect for its current inhabitants, and consider whether human presence would be unfair to the other creatures. We expect other humans to give us the same courtesy. It wouldn't be fair if someone came into your neighborhood and decided to bulldoze your home to build their home. Liberators don't believe in treating their brothers and sisters any differently.

As far as the animals are concerned, it doesn't matter why their homes are destroyed. The issue is that they cannot eat, sleep, play, walk, or raise a family in an area taken over by humans. And humans will take over land for more than building projects. **Ski slopes** are on clear cut mountain tops. **Mining** not only levels mountains and buries the area in tailings. It also pollutes waterways, extending its destruction for miles. **Utility easements**, making way for power and telephone lines, cut wide tracts of wilderness out of existence, so that metal monsters can march across the landscape. The **lumber** industry rapes forests and desertifies once pristine lands.

Perhaps the greatest exploitation of land is caused by the **grazing of domestic animals**, such as cattle and sheep. It is becoming common knowledge that rainforests are being cleared largely for the grazing of cattle. But the issue is bigger than it seems at first sight. Wild animals are destroyed, along with their habitat, to feed domestic animals, and these domestic animals are then slaughtered for human consumption.

In the United States the situation is just as bad. Huge areas of wilderness are destroyed to make way for cattle grazing. In addition, a **predator control program**, paid for with tax money, kills millions of animals each year who may in some way impact on the profitability of the ranching operation. This predator control program traps, poisons, and shoots many animal beings, including foxes, wolves, bobcats, mountain lions, raccoons, badgers, coyotes, mink, muskrat, hawks, eagles, and any other wildlife considered a nuisance to ranchers. But traps and poisons are not specific to "target animals". Casualties to non-target birds, small mammals, and even domestic dogs and cats, are in the hundreds of thousands every year.

The predator control program is only one covert abuse associated with the animal flesh business. Another, bigger one is **the use of agricultural land to feed the billions of domestic animals that are to be slaughtered.** It takes sixteen pounds of quality vegetable protein to make one pound of animal flesh. This means that growing grain to feed animals who are ultimately consumed by carnivorous humans, stresses the land sixteen times more than it would to support vegetarians. When you consider that 90% of all grains harvested are fed to animals destined for slaughter, it becomes apparent how much agricultural land is devoted to satisfying our society's meat obsession.

To liberators, the significance of this is two fold. First, land used for agriculture is usurped for humans, when it could support wild life. If you were interested in acting fairly to animals when living in nature with them, you certainly wouldn't destroy their land to make it exploitable for agriculture, or produce food in excess of what was necessary for your survival.

Also, consider that **pesticides and herbicides** are religiously and liberally applied to these grains. The **chemical industry** is a tremendously powerful interest. Organic farming practices may be on the increase for direct consumer crops. But these constitute a minute portion of all crops grown. The majority of agribusiness's output goes to feeding animals. Fields are sprayed, and these poisons kill hundreds of thousands, if not millions, of field mice, rabbits, coyotes, hawks, and others who have managed to adapt to life in the few trees or bushes that line the farm lands.

One shouldn't forget that the more land that is in production, the more energy is consumed, contributing to the oil problem discussed above. Energy is always an implicit component of any operation, and its covert abuse of non-humans must not be overlooked.

The only energy source we have so far touched on is the oil industry, which includes oil drilling and shipping, as a killer of our family of creatures. **Nuclear reactors**, which release low levels of radiation into the environment, damage local wildlife. Liberators point out that if people living near nuclear reactors are coming down with higher levels of leukemia and other cancers, what do you think is happening to the millions of creatures who haven't the choice of living elsewhere? Also, water used to cool nuclear generators is heated and then returned to its source, usually a river, raising the temperature of the surrounding ecosystem. When the ecosystem changes, animals dependent on old conditions are destroyed.

Nuclear reactors are not alone in being hazardous to non-humans. **Hydroelectric plants** employ **dams** which alter the entire ecosystem of huge expanses of land. Deserts become lakes, and rivers downstream dry up to a trickle so that they can only support a fraction of the beings that had come to rely on their life giving waters.

No discussion of the damage to nature and its animals by the energy production system would be complete without mentioning the burning of **coal** and its consequent production of acid rain. Lakes have become barren waters, and forests have been reduced to brown, lifeless rubble by the effects of acid rain. Where did the millions upon millions of animals who inhabited those lakes and forests go?

Liberators sadly accept that people don't think about the effects of their energy consumption on nonhuman beings. Who wants to see that when they turn on a light, they turn off a life?

These comments have not been meant to delve into the details of each of these aspects of society. They were to present the basic reasons why liberators see society as irreversibly corrupt. Liberators use this argument to demonstrate that **all who participate in this system are up to their necks in the blood of innocent creatures.** Even the most avid animal lover is guilty of murder by participating in an evil, destructive system.

Liberators want people to know that all the protests, writing of Congressmen, and payment of dues to animal protection organizations

will not cancel the fact that they are paying for animal research in medicine and the military, the predator control program, subsidies to the logging industry, price supports to grain farmers, the maintenance of public lands used by hunters, the building and maintenance of highways, the defense of oil industry investments, and many more animal abuses with their tax dollars.

The next time you give a $10 donation to an animal organization, think about the thousands of dollars you annually give through income, sales and property taxes to support animal cruelty.

Liberators illustrate the irony of living in an animal abusive system as an animal lover by referring to the care of companion animals. Some people have accepted the moral necessity of living as strict vegetarians, which, by the way, is a minority position even among those who call themselves "animal rights activists". Yet many of these devout vegetarians open a tin of cat or dog food to feed their companions a dinner of chicken, cow, or fish flesh. **How can anyone proclaim a love for animals, but kill one type of animal to feed another, liberators wonder?**

The answer has invariably come back that dogs and cats are not naturally vegetarian, so feeding them meat is allowing them to live according to their normal tendencies. To liberators, this answer ignores the fact that dogs and cats are domesticated creatures, alienated from their natural states. Their eating habits cannot be justified on the basis of wild animal behavior. Also, when carnivores kill they do so as an amoral act. When a cat or dog kills, it is not an evil deed, committed from immoral intentions. It is what these animals do. When humans kill cows to feed cats and dogs, it is an intentional, premeditated act, and therefore has moral dimensions. **Why choose the dog and cat over the cow?**

Each time someone opens a container of pet food, they are feeding their companions the flesh of innocent creatures killed for speciesist reasons. It is a conscious choice of helping one species of animals over another. This time the speciesism is not manifested in a choice of humans over all other beings. Rather, it is a choice of certain species of non-humans over others. It's a little broader minded, perhaps, but speciesism, nonetheless.

Cats and dogs can be kept healthy on strict vegetarian diets, as some people have discovered. But feeding dogs and cats a vegetarian diet takes effort. The **multi-billion dollar pet food industry**, which is closely connected with the slaughter house business, capitalizes on the compassion of short sighted people who like companion animals. The pet food industry supports the **pet store industry**, which supports the **breeding industry**. All this is paid for by participants in the system, who buy pet food to feed "their" animals. Such participants could be animal researchers or little old lady animal lovers.

You may be having difficulty swallowing the liberator position presented in this chapter. Liberators are concerned that people exposed to these ideas may be stressed beyond their tolerance limit, causing them to close off to liberator ideas completely. After all, liberators are saying that everyone who participates in this mad, abusive, murderous system is guilty of the slaughter of innocent beings. That's a heavy rap to take, especially if you think of yourself as a compassionate person. You will probably conclude that you have no choice but to participate in society, hoping to ease your conscience by saying it is out of your control. **How can you live without a car, or without using electricity generated by abusive means, or without buying consumer products shipped by killer vehicles, or without paying your taxes?** You can't be part of this society, keep your job, raise your family, and go on living a normal life if you were as extreme as liberators suggest you be.

How can you pay your membership dues to organizations, drive to rallies, write your Congressmen, and feed your dog if you can't abuse some animals along the way?

"Maybe some abuse is necessary to keep on working within the system to end abuse?" you may ask.

The liberators' answer to that is **"bullshit!" To liberators, when someone works within the system it is a choice.** If his reason for staying in the system is to fight for his family, liberators would understand. That's what they believe they are doing! Every war has infiltrators and saboteurs who help scatter the enemy's energy. **Liberators believe that most people, however, work within the system because they are consumers, just as society trained them to be.** They like driving cars, buying furniture, having a nice home, being respected members their community. **They work within the system because they want to be part of society. It's for them, not the animals.**

The covert nature of much animal abuse allows pseudo-conscientious people to fool themselves into believing that they can be members of this society and still be living a cruelty free life. Liberators hope their arguments have dispelled that myth. If they have, you are probably feeling depressed right now. To the liberators, that's good. **Pain tills the soil of change.** Once you are ready, liberators wish to plant a few seeds.

In short, liberators believe that animal abuse is an integral part of social reality. As social creatures manipulated by the abusive forces that be, we are accomplices to the assassination of our family of creatures. Combined with the limitations of human nature in respecting non-human life, a deadly, impenetrable barrier exists to the liberation of animals. **These people believe that only a revolution, the complete termination of this society, will enable us to save our family from torture and death.**

I will spend the next chapter discussing non-violence as a possible method for revolution. I will present the liberator explanation of why non-violence is not applicable to freeing animals, and explain why they believe militant intervention is the only effective alternative.

Chapter Five

THE MYTH OF NON-VIOLENCE

"What has been is what will be, and what has been done is what will be done; and there is nothing new under the sun."

The Bible's Ecclesiastes can be used for historical purposes to show that several thousand years ago, people were wrestling with the fact of human cruelty and the difficulty of finding an answer to it all. **How do we make sense out of the madness of the world we have created?** As said in the previous chapters, liberators believe human nature and society are never going to allow an ethic of respect for animals. **Given the liberator approach, then, how are true animal lovers going to live in this world? If your family is doomed to suffering and death, what can you do about it?**

"Again I saw all the oppressions that are practiced under the sun. And behold, the tears of the oppressed, and they had no one to comfort them! On the side of the oppressors there was power, and there was no one to comfort them. And I thought the dead who are already dead more fortunate than the living who are still alive, but better than both is he who has not yet been, and has not seen the evil deeds that are done under the sun."

The writer of Ecclesiastes was aware of evil, and realized that all human action to change evil into good was for naught. *"Vanity of vanities, says the Preacher, all is vanity."*

We cannot make a difference! We are kidding ourselves if we think we can. Liberators agree with that biblical author. But they disagree with his ultimate prescription for coping with the evil in the world. *"Fear God, and keep his Commandments; for this is the whole duty of man. For God will bring every deed into judgment, with every secret thing, whether good or evil."*

You can see the foundation of the peace movement in these quotations from the Bible. There is the recognition that evil exists, and a belief that God will judge all evil at some point. When you throw in the Christian ideal of turning the cheek and loving your enemy, you get the following strategy. Live peacefully, refrain from killing, and love the oppressors as your brothers, for all evil will be judged by God.

It seems like a tall order, asking humans to live like Jesus Christ. But the real meaning of this strategy is more true to human nature. **It means that you should cover your own ass by obeying God's commandments, so that when your day of judgment comes you will be a shoe in to Heaven. On the other hand, the evil oppressors will get theirs when God gets His hands on them.** In other words, let God do the dirty work of punishing evil bastards – keep your record clean! There is nothing wrong with punishment of oppressors, just with humans doing the punishing.

According to the liberators, that's not exactly loving ones oppressors!

Nothing is new under the sun. **People have oppressed others before, and freedom fighters have existed to oppose them.** Just as Christ's tactic was in the form of self suffering and preaching love for all, even for his oppressors, so have other social reformers sought love and peace as a force for social change.

Some people who hope to end the suffering and killing of animals are attracted to non-violence, for reasons, interpreted by liberators, that will become clearer near the end of this chapter. Their modern day hero is M. K. Gandhi. Some broader minded people use Dr. Martin Luther King Jr., as a model. Since King was essentially a Black American Christian clone of Gandhi, and himself quotes Gandhi on many occasions, the following analysis of non-violent resistance will concentrate on the originator of the modern day peace movement – and with his own words. Let's look at Gandhi's non-violent resistance and see what his approach was all about. The following analysis will use Gandhi's book, *Non-Violent Resistance*, published by Schocken Books (all emphasis is added). As in other chapters, this presentation is from the point of view of liberators.

The main force that Gandhi used was called Satyagraha, also called passive resistance. Satyagraha is a word that he coined, and it means soul force, or truth force. At its root is the view that: *"[one's opponent] must be weaned from error by patience and sympathy. For what means truth to one may be error to the other. And patience means self-suffering. So the doctrine came to mean vindication of truth not by infliction of suffering on the opponent but on one's self."* One key point of Satyagraha is that, *"It excludes the use of violence because* **man is not capable of knowing the absolute truth and, therefore, not competent to punish.** *"* If one punishes oneself, then errors in judgment would not hurt others. As Gandhi explained: *"Everybody admits that sacrifice of self is infinitely superior to sacrifice of others. Moreover, if this kind of force is used in a cause that is unjust, only the person using it suffers. He does not make others suffer for his mistakes. Men have before now done many things which were subsequently found to have been wrong. It is therefore meet [sic] that he should not do that which he knows to be wrong, and suffer the consequences whatever it may be. This is the key to the use of soul-force."*

To illustrate the effectiveness of using soul-force, Gandhi told of one of the *"sweetest recollections in his life"* in which it was used . His wife, Kasturba, was suffering from a hemorrhagic malady and seemed refractory to usual forms of treatment. Gandhi felt that she should abstain from eating salt and pulses to purify her body as a treatment. Asking her to give up pulses and salt was like asking the average American to give up meat. Let's have Gandhi tell the rest of the story.

"At last she challenged me saying that even I could not give up these articles if I was advised to do so. I was pained and equally delighted – delighted in that I got an opportunity to shower my love on her. I said to her: 'You are mistaken. If I was ailing and the doctor advised me to give up these or any other articles I should unhesitatingly do so. But there! Without any medical advice, I give up salt and pulses for one year, whether you do so or not.

"She was rudely shocked and exclaimed in deep sorrow: 'Pray forgive me. Knowing you, I should not have provoked you. I promise to abstain from these things, but for heaven's sake take back your vow. This is too hard on me.'

"'It is very good for you to give up these articles. I have not the slightest doubt that you will be all the better without them. As for me, I cannot retract a vow seriously taken. And it is sure to benefit me, for all restraint, whatever prompts it, is wholesome for man. You will therefore leave me alone. It will be a test for me, and a moral support to you in carrying out your resolve.'

"So she gave me up. 'You are too obstinate. You will listen to none'she said, and sought relief in tears."

Gandhi called this an example of domestic Satyagrahi. It's key elements are the same for all forms of this technique.

Notice that, much like a child who holds his breath until turning blue, Gandhi engaged in self-suffering to get what he wanted. **He played on another's love and pity.** As he said: *"Force of love and pity are greater than the force of arms."* In other words, give others a guilt trip. Say to them: "If you don't do what I want I'll hurt myself, and it will be on your conscience."

It is extremely important that the ones to whom you apply self-suffering tactics have a conscience. The basis of the technique is that others will learn the truth you are trying to communicate as they empathize with your pain and suffering. **Empathy and identification are essential for self-suffering to work.**

To have empathy and identification, there must be a sense of oneness between individuals, and a mutual love. Gandhi referred to this in the term *ahimsa*, which is a universal love. But it is a typical Eastern religion term, with many nuances of meaning foreign to Western minds. For example, it means dissociating oneself from all worldly possessions and relationships (marriage is out for true people with ahimsa – you are not supposed to play favorites). In this context, ahimsa is the realization of a kinship with all people, and, in fact, with all animals.

Gandhi gave an example of the power of ahimsa and non-violence associated with it in dealing with a thief:

"You set this armed robber down as an ignorant brother; you intend to reason with him at a suitable opportunity; you argue that he is, after all, a fellow man; you do not know what prompted him to steal. You, therefore, decide that, when you can, you will destroy the man's motive for stealing. Whilst you are thus reasoning with yourself, the man comes again to steal. Instead of being angry with him you take pity on him. You think that this stealing habit must be a disease with him. Henceforth, you, therefore, keep your doors and windows open, you change your sleeping-place, and you keep your things in a manner most accessible to him. The robber comes again and is confused as all this is new to him; nevertheless, he takes away your things. But his mind is agitated. He inquires about you in the village, he comes to learn about your broad and loving heart, he repents, he begs your pardon, returns your things, and leaves off the stealing habit. He becomes your servant, and you will find for him honorable employment."

Yea, right, Gandhi, exclaim the liberators! Even social workers don't believe that crap about people.

Gandhi was probably only talking about Indians, not Americans or other Western peoples. In fact, he did say that his experiment in non-violent resistance had the best chance of working in India. And he said, near the end of his life, **"I am but a poor mortal. I believe in my experiment and in my uttermost sincerity. But it may be that the only fitting epitaph after my death will be 'He tried but signally failed.'"**

Alas, Gandhi, all is vanity!

The above description of how to deal with a thief illustrates Gandhi's belief that: *"Three-fourth of the miseries and misunderstandings in the world will disappear, if we step into the shoes of our adversaries and understand their standpoint. We will then agree with our adversaries quickly or think of them charitably."* In other words, empathy will bring understanding and peace.

To be this ideal person, full of love and forgiveness, is to be a Satyagrahi, a practitioner of Satyagraha. This type of person is the Eastern equivalent of

Christic. *"He has to almost, if not entirely, be a perfect man."* **Gandhi did not think of himself or his followers as real Satyagrahis.**

This is what it takes to be a Satyagrahi, a true passive resistor. Gandhi made the following rules: (I quote)

1. A Satyagrahi, i.e., a civil resister will harbour no anger.

2. He will suffer the anger of the opponent.

3. In so doing he will put up with assaults from the opponent, never retaliate; but he will not submit, out of fear of punishment or the like, to any order given in anger.

4. When any person in authority seeks to arrest a civil resister, he will voluntarily submit to the arrest, and he will not resist the attachment or removal of his own property, if any, when it is sought to be confiscated by the authorities.

5. If a civil resister has any property in his possession as a trustee, he will refuse to surrender it, even though in defending it he might lose his life. He will however, never retaliate.

6. Non-retaliation excludes swearing and cursing.

7. Therefore, a civil resister will never insult his opponent, and therefore also not take part in many of the newly coined cries which are contrary to the spirit of ahimsa.

8. A civil resister will not salute the Union Jack, nor will he insult it or officials, English or Indian.

9. In the course of the struggle if any one insults an official or commits an assault upon him, a civil resister will protect such official or officials from the insult or attack even at the risk of his life.

Those were Gandhi's words. I have not exaggerated them.

What may seem strange was Gandhi's insistence that **non-violence resistance is only possible when those resisting are absolutely loyal to the State.** Gandhi got this idea from Thoreau, who coined the term **civil disobedience**. It is the belief that a man of honor, who normally obeys moral laws, has a right to disobey immoral laws. As Gandhi said: *"The privilege of resisting or disobeying a particular law or order accrues only to him who gives willing and unswerving obedience to the laws laid down for him."*

Unless all moral laws are obeyed scrupulously, the resister is ineffective. This is because **public opinion is tremendously important in this non-resistance approach.** *"Experience has shown that mere appeal to the reason produces no effect upon those who have settled convictions. The eyes of their understanding are opened not by argument but by the suffering of the Satyagrahi. The Satyagrahi strives to reach reason through the heart. The method of reaching the heart is to awaken public opinion. Public opinion for which one cares is a mightier force than that of gunpowder."* If the Satyagrahi was not pure of mind, spirit, and action, if he was not a model human being, then it would weaken the pity that the public would feel at his suffering.

Liberators hold that whenever a theory seems too naive to stand on its own, you can bet God isn't far behind. Naïveté in theory becomes faith in God. Gandhi's theory is no exception.

He believed that a faith in God is essential for non-violent resistance. *"A Satyagrahi has nothing to do with victory. He is sure of it, but he has also to know that it comes from God. His is but to suffer."*

When asked whether Socialists or Communists could be Satyagrahis, Gandhi explained: *"I'm afraid not. For a Satyagrahi has no other stay but God, and he who has any other stay or depends on any other help cannot offer Satyagraha... I am talking of those who are prepared in the name of God to stake their all for the sake of their principle... To bear all kinds of tortures without a murmur of resentment is impossible for a human being without the strength that comes from God. Only in His strength we are strong. And only those who can cast their cares and their fears on that immeasurable Power have faith in God."*

Suffering and dying make sense if there is a God to pass judgment on it all. Haven't Christians heard that message before? The writer of Ecclesiates was correct: there is nothing new under the sun.

Gandhi's plan of using Satyagraha in dealing with oppression was starkly stated in his discussion of the German Jews'struggle with Nazi Germany:

"Can the Jews resist this organized and shameless persecution? Is there a way to preserve their self-respect, and not to feel helpless, neglected and forlorn? I submit there is. No person who has faith in a living God need feel helpless or forlorn... As the Jews attribute personality to God and believe that He rules every action of theirs, they ought not to feel helpless. If I were a Jew and were born in Germany and earned my livelihood there, I would claim Germany as my home even as the tallest gentile German may, and challenge him to shoot me or cast me in the dungeon: I would refuse

to be expelled or to submit to discriminating treatment... If the Jewish mind could be prepared for voluntary suffering, even the massacre I have imagined could be turned into a day of thanksgiving and joy that Jehovah had wrought deliverance of the race even at the hands of the tyrant. For the God-fearing, death has no terror. It is a joyful sleep to be followed by a waking that would be all the more refreshing for the long sleep."

Liberators doubt whether the multitudes of activists who speak in favor of Gandhi's approach and its application to the animal movement have ever read his writings. Let's examine some of the details of non-violent resistance and, given the liberator perspective, see its inappropriateness for freeing animals from human oppression.

First, **his approach demanded a purity and perfection of soul that even highly spiritual people, such as Gandhi's followers, had not even achieved.** It required that one give up all worldly possessions, too. *"The use of Satyagraha requires the adoption of poverty, in the sense that we must be indifferent whether we have the where withal to feed or clothe ourselves."*

Does this mean that activists must give up their jobs, cars, and homes, and live simply by their faith that God would provide? Gandhi expected his civil resisters to do so. *"No civil resister is to expect maintenance for his dependents. It would be an accident if any such provision is made. A civil resister entrusts his dependents to the care of God."* But don't worry. Gandhi continued: *"It is the universal experience that in such times hardly anybody is left to starve."*

Civil resisters do not pay taxes that support the evil system. They all practice non-cooperation, which is the mildest form of Satyagraha. This entails the withdrawal from society. Gandhi outlined some basic steps to be taken as the first stage of non-cooperation: (I quote)

1. Surrender of all tittles of honor and honorary offices.

2. Non-participation in Government loans.

3. Suspension by lawyers of practice and settlement of civil disputes by private arbitration.

4. Boycott of Government schools by parents.

5. Non-participation in Government parties, and such other function.
While some of these prescriptions for non-cooperation were designed for the Indian problem, their intent was clear. **Thoreau**, in his essay, On the

duty of Civil Disobedience, a work which highly influenced Gandhi, said: *"I do not hesitate to say, that those who call themselves abolitionists should at once effectually withdraw their support, both in person and property, from the government of Massachusetts, and not wait till they constitute a majority of one, before they suffer the right to prevail through them."*

Thoreau also quoted **Confucius**, who said: ***"If a State is governed by the principles of reason, poverty and misery are subjects of shame; if the State is not governed by the principles of reason, riches and honors are the subjects of shame."***

Indeed, nothing is new under the sun! **From Confucius, to Thoreau, to Gandhi the message has been that participation in an unjust system must stop for those who want to change that system.**[5] What does that mean for those wanting to free the animals?

It means that you can't afford the plane tickets to the next march in Washington, DC. If you think about it, you were welcome business for airlines, hotels, taxicabs, and other tourist services. How many thousands of dollars of taxes were raised through animal activist purchases, from airline tickets to soft drinks? What abuses of animals do you think that money will go towards?

The typical person concerned about animals is white, middle class, and not about to give up property, titles, or wealth. Even the animal rights groups are deeply entrenched in the system. Many national animal organizations have millions of dollars, which they invest in stocks, bonds, or real estate. **This isn't non-participation with society.**

Professions capitalize on their credentials to gain public respect, as when "MD's" speak out against animal research. **This isn't exactly surrendering all titles of honor or honorary offices!**

The fact is, no one in this society who proclaims a belief in non-violent resistance practices anything like true Satyagraha. Does it make a difference? It does if they are supporting Gandian tactics. **Liberators believe that so long as people participate in the society which they condemn, they are nothing more than hypocrites.**

The point here is that Gandian non-violent resistance demands that resisters behave in a self-sacrificial, self-denying manner. People in Western society just don't behave that way. Gandhi found that they don't necessarily behave that way in Eastern society, either. This is one reason why liberators believe non-violent resistance is inappropriate as a model.

The second reason they believe Gandhi's approach is inappropriate for the animal liberation movement has to do with his appraisal of human nature, which is central to his philosophy and approach. **He believed that humans are basically good.** If you show them you are suffering because of their actions, then they will feel pity and change their ways. He also believed that oppressors lose all pleasure in their actions when the victim betrays no resistance. *"The wrong-doer wearies of wrong doing in the absence of resistance."*

You might agree with Gandhi's assessment of human nature. You might even, like Gandhi, make stealing easy for the thief, so as to reform him. **But the success of that approach depends on the ability of victimizers to empathize with their victims.** Perhaps in a small village, with mostly well intentioned people, such an approach could work. **But liberators remind us to get back to reality – late 20th century, animal abusing reality.**

People see animals as exploitable objects. They eat them, something that the British didn't do to the Indians (at least not in public). **The level of respect for animal life is so low, as outlined in the previous chapter, that a reliance on human empathy for non-humans is more than naive – it is destructive to animals.** Furthermore, over the millennia during which animals have been butchered by people for one reason or another, their **oppressors have never grown weary of their deeds of terror, *despite animal non-resistance*.** If anything, domestication has led to strains of animals which are more easily manipulated than older ones, making the slaughter even simpler for humans to perform.[6]

Gandhi was dealing with the sensibilities of humans towards humans. Guilt, or pity, only work when there is a connection between oppressor and oppressed. Gandhi gambled that even the most blind oppressor would eventually stop his aggression when he met unselfish, pure, non-violent resisters.

Liberators ask who is a better non-violent resistor than a dog about to be experimented on, sitting helplessly in a cage at a laboratory, or a cow anxiously waiting in a feed lot to be slaughtered? Animals are the ultimate Satyagrahis! They have no possessions, they do not participate in the system, and, despite their abuses, they still have the capacity to love humans. Some, like dogs, can even love those who abuse them. Kick them and they will apologize for hurting your foot. Gandhi would have been proud of such self-suffering creatures.

Despite their cries, blood, and dead bodies, people are unmoved. Liberators are not surprised by this. As explained earlier, they believe that **empathy is essential for pity to work, and animals receive little empathy from humans.**

Liberators feel that people who support non-violence are confusing the objects of oppression with the agents of liberation. Gandhi's Satyagrahis were both the oppressed and the liberators. **When it comes to animals, humans can merely act as the agents of liberation.** Humans can vicariously suffer for animals. The oppressors will see this human suffering as vicarious. But if oppressors have no respect for animals, will their hearts be melted into compassion by seeing other humans suffering for them? Of course not, say the liberators!

When people have no empathy for animals, they see humans who have empathy foranimals as lunatics. Telling a vivisector that you love rats is like telling him you love rocks. If you fasted and engaged in all sorts of self-suffering to demonstrate the truth that you hold about animals needing to be free, then the oppressors will pity you – as mad!

This, then, is one problem the animal movement has that Gandhi's civil rights movement did not have. The liberators are not the same as the liberated. Humans have sympathy and pity for other humans (sometimes), but they will not necessarily extend that sympathy and pity to rats, mice, goats, pigs and dogs. Remember, it is important that the ones towards whom you apply self-suffering have a conscience. Unless people have a conscience about the way they deal with animals, which most people do not have, human self-suffering will never get the job done of raising consciousness.

There is another problem which occurs when a human acts as an agent for the animals. According to liberators, there is a different responsibility being an agent for someone else, than merely acting as one's own agent. If it is your own life under fire, you can use non-violent tactics if you wish. You have a right to attend your own funeral! But what if it isn't your own life for which you are responsible?

People practice non-violence for personal reasons. It is a way of life, a strategy for dealing with the world. When acting as an agent for others, however, a dogmatic adherence to non-violence can work against the best interests of the individuals being protected. Liberators assert that a good agent must do whatever is necessary to protect his wards. This means that one's personal preferences regarding non-violence may have to be overridden if the circumstances demand it.

For example, consider a situation in which ten innocent children are about to be slaughtered by an insane killer. Anon-violent woman has accepted the responsibility for protecting the children. She does everything peaceful that she possibly can imagine to stop the massacre. Unfortunately, her efforts are useless. While she could stop the man with force, she rejects such intervention. He lifts a machete and prepares to decapitate the first child, who is bound and gagged. Watching the slaughter, she prays to God for the children's and murderer's deliverance. A few moments later the children are all dead, and the murderer leaves the scene to terrorize and destroy other lives.

In this situation, non-violence may have made the protector feel virtuous. But it resulted in the death of the children, whose protection was her responsibility. **Liberators believe that non-violence may be chosen as a personal way of life, but it makes for lousy protectors.**

In short, it is fine to risk one's own life with non-violence. But do not endanger others in need of physical intervention by declaring yourself their savior.

Liberators say it's animal abuse when non-violent animal supporters allow animals to die simply because these self-appointed guardians value non-violence over fighting for the animal's lives and liberty.

Gandhi said that human uncertainty is a root cause for accepting a strategy of non-violence, since we have no right to inflict our potentially erroneous assessments on others. The purpose of non-violence, then, is to live by your own beliefs and let others live by theirs. Hopefully, as others see you suffering because of their oppressive behaviors, they will come around to seeing things your way. But when you are agents of animals who are being slaughtered by the millions daily, can you take such a live and let live attitude?

Liberators make their point angrily. **Not intervening to protect animals is to allow crimes against our wards to take place. Indeed, it is a live and let die attitude to accept non-violence in the struggle for animal freedom. The animals need us to save them. Let us not inflict our mistaken belief, the liberators say, in accepting non-violence to keep animals from receiving our help**.

Despite these arguments, some readers may still reject the use of force to stop animal abusers. Liberators consider some people dogmatically committed to a pacifist position when it comes to saving animals. The dilemma for these conscientious objectors, who consider themselves protectors of the animals, is easy to resolve, as far as liberators are concerned. **If you feel it is wrong to use force to stop animal abuse, that's fine. Just don't consider yourself a protector of animals. Innocent members of our family are being abused and killed en masse. The animals don't need people who are afraid of asserting, in a physically meaningful way, that such treatment of our family is wrong and must stop.**

Those readers who have studied Gandhi may object to the implication that Satyagrahis only fought for their own liberation. In fact, there were times when Gandhi used Satyagrahis as instruments for other social change, acting on behalf of other disenfranchised groups. One example was their efforts in gaining equality for the "Untouchables," a caste of people not allowed near temples or on temple roads, and who generally were treated "like animals". Some people might reason that the Satyagrahis acting on behalf of the "Untouchables" is the equivalent of humans acting on behalf of the animals. Can this then justify non-violent resistance for the animal liberation movement?

Consider Gandhi's reflections on the "Untouchable" liberation campaign. He thought the "Untouchables" needed social reform, rather than political reform. On this difference, he observed, *"I have long believed that social is a tougher business than political reform. The atmosphere is ready for the latter, people are interested in it... On the other hand, **people have little interest in social reform, the result of agitation does not appear to be striking** and there is little room for congratulations and addresses. **The social reformers will have therefore to plod on for some time, hold themselves in peace, and be satisfied with apparently small results.** "*

The common feature of the "Untouchable" struggle with the animal liberation struggle is that one group is acting on behalf of another. In one, Satyagrahis acted on behalf of "Untouchables," and in the other, humans act on behalf of the other creatures. The difference is that the "Untouchables" are still human. To analogize the two struggles is an error.

Despite having this human advantage, Gandhi recognized that the process will be slow and arduous. In fact, the "Untouchables" still suffer in India. **Why was he willing to accept such small results of non-violent resistance?**

Partly, the liberators say, it is because God will have the final say on justice. I will return to that in a moment. But it is also because **Gandhi expected the people who are resisting, and the group that they are representing, to always remain a part of the society they are fighting.** That opinion is even made clear in his advice to Jews, telling them they should not leave Germany, but should stay and accept their nationality and convert their oppressors with love.

Liberators recognize this as a critical feature of non-violent resistance. It assumes that the resistors, and the groups they represent, ultimately want to live with the people who are now their oppressors. That is why non-violent resistors are to obey all laws rigorously, except for the immoral ones. They are to be model citizens, showing that it is out of loyalty to country and love for others that they suffer. This approach considers it better to accept small moves in the right direction, than risk alienating society in an attempt at getting more. Remember, alienation is the opposite of identification, which is needed for empathy. In order for non-violence to work, the oppressors need to feel connected to their victims. In that way the victims' suffering will cause suffering in the oppressors.

Gandhi was trying to get people included in the power structure of Indian society. It was a movement of inclusion. If you get inclusion through violence, then it will always be an uneasy relationship. True love between people can only be reached by peaceful means. This was essentially Gandhi's position. Liberators say Gandhi may have been correct, as far as humans living with other humans are concerned, although they have less faith in human nature than he. But correct or not, they feel his point is irrelevant for the animal movement.

Liberators are not working for the inclusion of animals in society. They are working to free animals from human interference in their lives. From the animals' point of view, they contend, it doesn't matter why animals are left alone, so long as they are. Having a loving revolution is only important if you want to be around afterwards to love one another. Animals don't want human love, only freedom from human exploitation. 7

So long as humans are the agents of the animals, however, liberators see a problem. **The animals need freedom, but their human agents are concerned about living with other humans.** To put it bluntly, **humans have a conflict of interest when they help animals.**8 This is because humans are part of the society which abuses animals. They want to get along with other humans. Every animal supporter wishes that the world consisted of other animal respecting humans with whom they could live peacefully, in harmony with the other animals. Yet, the society in which humans live will never stop abusing other creatures, and, in fact, has become invested in continuing that abuse.

Liberators contend there is no way that people will stop eating flesh, driving cars, wearing leather, hunting, and doing all other overt and covert abuses of animals simply because a handful of "lunatics" feel compassion for beasts. Even Gandhi admits that you can't get through to everyone. When it comes to animals, liberators say you can't get through to most of the people in the world.

What is the conscientious animal defender to do?

The liberator solution is the use of physical force. They believe force is a necessary method for defending animal beings against their human being oppressors. The fact that we are human need not stop us. But it does demand, they say, that each person reassess his or her loyalties.

If you are of the family of all creatures, brother or sister to the other animals, then you must stop cooperation with society and participating in the slaughter, and fight for your family.

If you are of the family of man, then don't call yourself an agent or defender of the animals. You have a conflict of interest, and not admitting it is doing animals more harm than good. It can mislead people who are of the family of creatures, and who may be willing to fight for their family.

People who are of the family of man engage in tactics which are designed more to keep peace with other people than to free the animals. This is why most animal organizations are concerned more about public opinion than their effectiveness in liberating animals.

The liberators haven't finished with Gandhi, yet. Let's return to Gandhi's other answer to the problem of facing impossible obstacles. He believed God is there to rescue the suffering and bind their wounds – even unto death.

Agreeing with the writer of Ecclesiastes, Gandhi proposed that the way to deal with life's cruel reality is, in common parlance, to let go and let God. As with all religious positions, there is no way to argue against this belief.

Liberators lament that the power of God is not in God itself, but in the impenetrable wall of faith His name invokes.

They point out that a mouse about to be scalded by boiling water in the name of science is not comforted by a human's belief in God. To rely on divine judgment is a cop out. If he could, maybe the mouse would ask the researcher how he could believe in a god that would allow such cruelty to continue!

Gandhi and people in the New Age movement who are influenced by Eastern religions, have an answer for the mouse. The purpose of animal suffering is to provide sensitive humans with opportunities for growth. It is all a learning experience, helping us raise our consciousness and love for others. Gandhi even believed that life's evils were planned by God to test us.

Can you see how human centered such thinking is, ask the liberators? The world's problems are here as a test for us! **Tell the mouse that she**

is dying, not for science, but for a test of the moral fiber of human beings.

Liberators do not object to the belief that life's natural disasters are opportunities for personal growth. But are they planned for our growth? To regard them as such is to see the world and all its inhabitants as a resource for humans, objects placed in our way as obstacles to be overcome in the process of personal growth. It is another variant on the age old theme of anthropocentrism.

It is clear to liberators that non-violence will not work for the animal liberation movement. Yet, people still insist on its use. Why do people hold onto non-violence as a tactic when it is so clearly inappropriate?

Liberators ask that you face the truth. In their assessment, most people are cowards. They are comfortable sitting on their fat sofas, sipping beers, and watching football games on television. If a person likes dogs or cats, he may give twenty bucks to some animal group, particularly one that sends pictures of dogs and cats being experimented on. It's easy for some people to disagree with animal research. They don't have to change their behaviors, like the food they eat, or the fact that they drive through the living rooms of animals each day. Of course, they still want their prescription drugs when they are sick, even if the drug company does test them on animals.

Complacent people like this, who constitute the majority of people in this society, are too lazy and unthreatened in their own lives to engage in any real struggle for the animals. The civil rights movements in India and in this country were all by the people for the people. Indians fought for independence from the British, women fought for equality to men, blacks fought for the enforcement of their constitutional rights, gays fought for equality among straights, retired citizens fought to retain their power in society. And these struggles continue. **They are struggles of people wanting power in society. They are self-serving enterprises. And they only occur when a group of people feels threatened and oppressed enough to rise up against their oppressors.**

The animal liberation movement is entirely different, say the liberators. **It takes courage and conviction to fight for someone else's freedom when you are free yourself.** Most people don't have what it takes. So they hide their lack of courage and commitment behind a trust in God, or vows of non-violence.

There is another difference between human civil rights movements and the animal liberation movement. While no civil rights movement has been totally without the loss of lives, the level of carnage suffered by the animals is infinitely greater than anything experienced by humans. Thousands of people may die in their cause for liberty; but **billions** of animals are systematically, thoughtlessly, and brutally exterminated every year, which translates into millions each day! **Animals are bred for slaughter, fed for slaughter, and led to slaughter. The level of oppression experienced by animals is greater, more pervasive, and longer in existence than any human oppression against other humans. For people to fight on such a bloody battlefield for their fellow creatures takes great courage and conviction. Few humans have what it takes.**

Liberators think the animal exploiters know this sad fact about people. That's why so many conversations with animal abusers end with the abusers saying: "I'll respect your right to live according to your beliefs, but I expect you to respect my right to live according to mine." What they are saying is that we humans are entitled to an honest disagreement over choice of lifestyles. But let's not get too serious about this animal business.

Imagine how it would sound if they said: "I expect you to respect my right to treat your brothers and sisters as mine to use as I wish." You wouldn't merely shake hands and agree to disagree.

But, liberators say, that is exactly what happens each time a debate between animal abusers and animal supporters is conducted. Be peaceful and respectful at all cost. Don't get the public thinking that you are a bunch of violent fanatics. You have to live with your neighbors, even if they are animal exploiters, don't you?

Abusers know what choices most people will make. People have made them in the past. Abusers know there is nothing new under the sun. Most people will never put their lives on the line for animals. They do want to ease their consciences concerning animal suffering, but still participate in the cruel system.

Liberators have learned from personal experience that it's hard living in a cruel society as a participant, while trying to maintain a sensitivity to animals. In fact, as Confucius knew, it is impossible for a moral person to live in an immoral society.

For example, how can you eat in a restaurant as an animal supporter, when all the restaurants, except the handful of vegan ones in this country, are serving members of your family on platters with assorted sauces? How can you shop in a grocery store, when an entire department is devoted to selling body parts of your loved ones? The more sensitive you are to animals, the more difficult this participation becomes.

Liberators declare that the idea of non-violence as an effective means of gaining freedom for animals is a myth, perpetuated by people invested in making life in a cruel society easier for humans. The myth is promoted by four different factions in society. One is the abusers, invested in maintaining control over the oppressed. They prefer sign carrying, hymn singing protesters to bomb throwing, gun shooting liberators, and for obvious reasons. If the peaceful protesters feel their signs and songs are doing some good, then the protest will vent their anger and hostility to animal abuse, allowing them to blow off steam. This will keep them from engaging in more serious, violent, and effective action.

The second faction promoting the myth consists of moderate animal lovers. These people stand to lose whenever the status quo is upset, but they are uncomfortable with all features of the existing regime. They see non-violence and compromise as the best means for maintaining their comfortable lifestyles, while at the same time assuaging their consciences. Cowards and insincere people always prefer non-violence to physical intervention. Talk is always cheaper than action.

The third group is the religious people who believe that God will punish the sinners and reward the virtuous. They essentially pass the buck to the big man upstairs, and speak words of love and peace to make themselves seem pure and holy when their time comes up for judgment. To these people, non-violence helps them get to heaven, which is more important to them than helping other creatures get free from human bondage.

The fourth faction consists of "New Age" peaceniks, who style themselves according to their Westernized, oversimplified interpretation of Gandian non-violence. They believe that no peace can come from war, a point which Gandhi espoused. Like the religious people who want to leave judgment to God to keep their personal records clean, these spiritually minded people want to leave everything to karma and maximize their personal growth. They do not reflect on the inappropriateness of their tactics to animal liberation, because they are too busy reflecting on their own spiritual enlightenment and development. They may see the animal movement as a branch of their own growth in becoming more peaceful and loving people. Their interest in animals is secondary to their interest in becoming loving beings. When animals are being abused, they will speak out for love and peace, but will do nothing to physically stop the abuse. Sometimes, they are not even willing to face the destruction that exists all around them, since they want to keep a positive outlook and "good vibrations" in their lives. Of course, the animals gain nothing by this fair weather, anthropocentric love. The animals need liberators, not people who stick their heads in the sand, denying that the world is filled with evil, horrible acts committed against innocent creatures.

The liberators content that every massive, successful movement was never exclusively peaceful, even when it was designed to be. Gandhi's movement was consistently associated with violence, despite Gandhi's appeals for peace. The black civil rights movement had Martin Luther King Jr., but it also had Malcolm X. There were peace marches, but there were also race riots and Black Panthers actions and threats. It is popular for non-violence supporters to accept credit for gains made in these movements. But would the gains have been made without the specter of violence, real and threatened? Gandhi, for example, had millions of followers eager to fulfill his every command. Despite his message of Satyagraha, Gandhi, and the British officials, knew that the possibility of violence breaking out was real. How much of Gandhi's influence was due to the officials' fear of this potential for violence?

Liberators hold that the use of militant intervention is the only way to make people conscious of the fact that they cannot continue to exploit other creatures. One can't raise consciousness until there is consciousness. People are unconscious to the pain and suffering of non-humans. They are only conscious of the pleasures and pains that directly affect their lives.

Liberators say it's time lovers of animals make abusers conscious of pain when they hurt our family members.

The author of Ecclesiastes says: *"For everything there is a season, and a time for every matter under heaven."* Specifically, turn your attention to six such times: *"A time to kill, and a time to heal; a time to love, and a time to hate; a time for war, and a time for peace."*

Liberators believe it is a time to physically stop human oppressors, and allow our brothers and sisters, and the environment in which they live, to heal; it is a time to love animals with deeds and not mere words, and a time to hate humans for their callousness, bigotry, and greed; and it is a time for war on humankind, and a time for peace in our hearts by freeing ourselves from this massive destruction machine called society, whose wheels turn with the blood, sweat, and tears of animals.

---

5. Liberators agree with the moral requirement that one should not participate in an immoral system. But they do not believe this is for the purpose of changing the system. They believe the system cannot be changed in any significant way. Non-participation is simply to remove oneself from the bloodshed, making sure one does not contribute to or support it.

6. The inability to empathize or identify with the environment will likewise prevent non-violence to work for the environmental movement, according to the liberators.

All the arguments against non-violence for liberating animals applies to the liberation of the environment. Only militancy directed at the agents of destruction – people – will be effective.

7. See page later for a discussion of the "pet" situation.

8. See page later for a discussion of the human need to be with other people

Chapter Six

A TIME FOR WAR

I have explained why liberators believe human nature and human societies are unalterably resistant to freeing animals and treating them with respect. I have shown why liberators believe that non-violent resistance is ineffective in freeing animals, and explained why liberators see physical force as the only road for saving some of our family members. Yet, despite all the reasoning presented thus far, I am quite certain that most readers still shun militant action against animal abusers, but may now be entertaining notions of violence against liberators.

Thoreau said: *"He who gives himself entirely to his fellow-men appears to them useless and selfish; but he who gives himself partially to them is pronounced a benefactor and philanthropist."* Liberators give themselves totally to the animals. They have no doubt that they will be pronounced useless and selfish by some people.

This is not because some of you do not agree with liberators. My feeling is that many of you do. But who wants to feel that their struggle is hopeless? Liberators explain the average animal defender's reluctance to raise arms against human oppression of other beings by saying that those people are invested in the system. They are not ready to declare war on humans. Don't make excuses, liberators say. Admit your priorities are more with staying a part of the system than in overthrowing it. Admit your conflict of interest. **But please don't criticize real liberators.**

Liberators enjoy talking to people who are brave, honest, and loving enough to place the interests of their family of creatures over their material and social comforts. When they do, they begin as follows: *"Welcome, friends. We have some human butt to kick!"*

First, they explain, let's get rid of that terrible term, "animal rights". They have used it in discussions for recognition purposes and because most people who consider themselves defenders of animals call themselves animal rights activists. But they see many problems with the term. One is that **rights imply a relationship.** When you have a right it means that, in your dealings with others, those others have an obligation to respect your autonomy. The concept was developed to define the limits of human interaction, making exploitation of people a crime.

It may seem that animal rights is just what we want. But do we want to see humans relating with animals? No, explain the liberators. **They want humans to leave animals alone.** They want humans to have nothing to do with non-humans. The concept of animal rights includes animals in the moral and political community. Mainstream animal rights activists often fight to get animal rights encoded in the law. The entire enterprise of gaining rights is an insecure, tenuous one, since laws are easily challenged and changed, and are seldom enforced. **Liberators want non-humans left out of the human community!** Remember, to them it is a movement for exclusion of animals from society, not inclusion.

Liberators also remind others that the concept of rights is also not *necessary* in order to respect another's autonomy. If God appeared, we would not have to give Her rights in order to leave Her alone. We would leave Her alone out of respect, or fear. We can treat other creatures the same way.

Further, the very term "animal" differentiates humans from non-humans. All labels create distinctions. But distinctions are based on differences, and empathy is based on identification, which implies similarities. When someone speaks of animal rights, as distinct from human rights, there is an implicit assumption that humans are not animals. A belief that there is a difference between humans and animals can only hamper the connection and identification necessary for moral behavior towards other creatures.

Another problem with the concept of animal rights is that rights are modeled after rules for human interaction. Philosophers in the movement argue for extending our respect for fellow humans to other animals in the name of consistency. While liberators believe they are correct given their assumptions, the implicit problem with their approach is that they are using human systems and beliefs to model how we should behave to all other creatures.

Essentially, animal rights philosophers argue that so long as we treat people with respect, we should treat animals with respect, as well. In a subtle way, then animals are dependent on human sensibilities concerning how to treat other humans. If we didn't treat fellow humans well, the argument for treating animals well would be lost. In fact, many key figures in the animal rights movement have argued that using animals, say in research, would be acceptable if humans were used in the same way. They are not against the exploitation of animals, only the unequal exploitation of animals and humans. **Animals are, therefore, not respected on their own behalf, but merely by logical extension of human respect for other humans. This is another variant of the anthropocentrism that plagues human thought and action, and angers liberators.**

Finally, **rights, legal or moral, are only as good as the intent of the people constrained to live by them.** Black Americans had the right to vote since the Civil War. But the enforcement of that right was missing until about 80 years later. Likewise, animals can be declared free tomorrow. However, societal enforcement of their freedom would never come, according to liberators.

The term liberators use instead of the animal rights movement is "The Liberation Movement". Those in the movement are, therefore, called *liberators,* as opposed to animal rights activists. Their focus is on human aggression and exploitation of others. The others need not justify their likeness to humans in order to gain rights. The burden is on humans to cease their aggression, not on animals to prove themselves worthy of respect. Implied in this is a naturocentric view of the world, dethroning humans from their self-justified tyranny over others.

Liberators shift their loyalties from the family of man, to the family of creatures, or from anthropocentrism to naturocentrism. It means they no longer automatically put people first, or feel ashamed to admit that they value some chickens and mice more than some humans.

Liberators believe their approach offers hope which traditional, human-centered movements do not. **To them, hope is possible, even in their recognition that humans will always be cruel so long as they exist. Why? Because they do not hope for impossible things, like changing society. They hope to free family members, not save the world.**

The example they like to use is the following. If you awaken one day to find that your house is burning down, you don't just sit there and cry about it. You get up and quickly rescue whatever living beings are still in the house, and run like hell. If you manage to save some lives, then you can feel successful, even if there were some members you couldn't manage to save. Saving as many lives as possible was your goal. The fire was not your fault, and feeling that you failed because there was a fire and some lives were lost is placing yourself in an unwinnable position, with undeserving blame.

When you define your task in terms of saving or healing humankind, you focus on the burning house. There is no way you can win. But when you accept that the house will burn, you can focus on the lives saved and feel good about what you have done.

The liberators' secret to keeping a positive outlook is to know that, no matter how abusive this world has become to animals, they have been able to rescue some from the blaze of human caused terror and death. They don't see every animal liberation, even small ones where only a few animals are freed, as a battle in an unwinnable war against human cruelty. They see each liberation as a war in itself, totally won each time a single creature is freed from human exploitation.

In this way, liberators can keep their hopes alive, not that people will somehow change their inherent propensity to abuse animals, but that one person, with the will to succeed, can free a mouse from a laboratory, or liberate a chicken from a factory farm. **Liberators believe they can win thousands of wars in their lifetimes. They believe they must, for the animals.**

Before continuing, I am sure some readers are confused about the liberator statement that humans are to leave animals alone, period. What about humans relating to companion animals, or other relationships between creatures in which humans are one participant?

The liberator position is clear. **All interactions with other creatures should be by mutual consent.** That means that we should not chain horses to plows, or keep cows confined and milk them, turning their bodies into milk producing machines, and then justify our exploitation by saying that we feed and care for them. These are examples of manipulation and human parasitism. Even horses who are ridden, and learn to accept their rider, had to first be "broken". All intelligent creatures can be trained to accept, and even masochistically enjoy, their oppression, as some human slaves learned to do. But this does not make their oppression any less of an abuse. When a slave accepts his enslavement, he is no less a slave. His spirit is merely broken.

Liberators realize that it takes sensitivity and empathy to deal with another creature on mutually acceptable terms. Humans have never developed those skills. Instead, they kill and exploit whomever they can, and domesticate, which means genetically enslave, certain creatures for special purposes, either for laying eggs, working, producing milk or meat, research, entertainment or companionship.

Companion animals are a difficult problem, the liberators believe, because we have a responsibility to them for having made them dependent on humans. We should allow each to live as they must, as freely and happily as possible. This usually means living in contact with humans, since they are dependent on us for their basic needs. **But this should be a temporary situation.**

Ideally, liberators want all domestic animals to be prevented from breeding, including dogs and cats. This would end their genetically programmed dependence. To perpetuate domesticated animal breeds is to continue their enslavement. **Humans have created mutant beings, animals who have become nearly as alienated from their original natures as we have from ours.** Therefore, humans must care for them while they are alive. But they must prevent their reproduction and terminate their enslavement to humans.

All this may sound crazy coming from lovers and fellow members of the family of creatures. If it does, you have not yet started thinking as a liberator, with a naturocentric perspective. **To liberators, all human relationships with other creatures are currently on human terms.** We have made ourselves into their kings. Even many animal lovers support the idea of human stewardship of the animals, trying to transform the Biblical injunction of human dominion, i.e. domination over animals, into a more acceptable concept. But a liberator sees all this as human-centered bullshit! **Stewardship and dominion both say we're better than other creatures. In both cases, humans have power over the other animals in the world. Everyone knows that power corrupts, and absolute power, such as that allegedly sanctioned by God, or gained through domestication, corrupts absolutely.**

Most people can't imagine relating to fellow creatures without being in control. However, free, equal relationships with fellow creatures are possible, and rewarding. **Other creatures are not naturally frightened of humans.** Such beings as birds, squirrel's, deer, raccoons, wolves, rabbits, fish, and myriad other members of our family happily accept us if we do not show them we are going to be their stewards or kings. If we lived as respecting equals with other creatures, liberators believe, then we would have many satisfying relationships with them. But they would be mutually agreeable relationships, something which man, in need of control, cannot seem to understand or accept.

It takes time to re-orient your thinking to understand the liberator. You may be accustomed to considering only other humans as yourfriends and family members. But look around you! To the liberator, every creature that walks, swims, crawls, or flies is a friend and part of the family. The plants, streams, mountains, fields, and lakes are the family's home. Liberators find their love there, among the beings they consider their true family.

Liberators offer some strategies for liberating animals. First, **they claim that those willing to defend animals constitute the most compassionate, empathic, and courageous section of society.** That is why they have chosen to sacrifice their personal comfort to assist their non-human family members.

Liberators use an analogy to explain their role in society. Many anthropologists and philosophers have compared society to an organism. The roadways that allow transportation is the circulatory system. The educational system is the brain. And so on. Given this analogy, who are these conscientious, empathic people?

They are the white blood cells!

White blood cells spend their lives fighting disease, infection, and decay in the body. They martyr themselves in the process of keeping the body going. That is what ethically minded, compassionate people have historically done. The bulk of humankind has abused itself and the environment, causing wars, destruction, and suffering. A few brave souls have existed in each generation to martyr themselves in the name of goodness, to keep the body of society going. These people have thrown themselves onto the wheels of the destructive machinery of society, slowing down the evil forces that continue to grind away at the world. Thanks to this small group of people who care about moral issues, and put their actions behind their words, society has limped on through the millennia. Unfortunately, their actions have helped to sustain society and its oppression of other creatures and the planet.

Liberators firmly believe the best thing that could happen to the Earth and all of its non-human inhabitants is that human societies come to an end, along with all people. Human caused destruction to the environment and to other creatures would end. The tyranny of humankind would be over. That is a cause for which liberators would gladly martyr themselves.

There are two strategies by which white blood cells can fight the body. One way is passive, the other active. The passive one is to withdraw from society. It means one does not work for the body as a white blood cell anymore. That leaves the body defenseless, even to its own toxins. When good people withdraw from society, the body becomes unable to fight disease, such as corruption, greed, and selfishness. It will be like a body without an immune system. Slowly, it will die. **By not participating in society, liberators help make its end come closer to a reality.**

It is difficult for some people, who care about human suffering and feel empathy for other people, to withdraw from society and let it demolish itself. These people are not thinking with a liberator perspective. Liberators consider humans to have no greater claim on sympathy and activism than the animals they abuse. In fact, they believe their victims deserve greater attention and concern.

Some compassionate people see cruel individuals as somehow mentally or spiritually ill. They feel these cruel people should be cared for, not ignored and left to suffer due to their own illness. On the other hand, these compassionate people would probably agree that a sociopathic criminal should be locked up and prevented from hurting others. **If we define ourselves as part of the family of creatures, as liberators do, humans**

who exploit animals are the same as sociopathic criminals. However, because there are so few liberators, and the cruelty is socially accepted and encouraged, liberators cannot lock these criminals up. Liberators can, however, withdraw their support from the social system.

The active strategy is the use of **militant interventionism**. Using the white blood cell analogy, this is like an autoimmune disease. It means that the white blood cells now regard the body as alien, and attack it as they do other agents of disease. With time, the white blood cells cripple the body and destroy its ability to survive.

What form does militant interventionism take? It is liberating an abused dog, chained constantly to a tree, from its human oppressor. It is breaking into a factory farm, damaging the equipment and cages, and freeing some of the animals. It includes all sorts of monkey wrenching, from disabling vehicles, to disabling roadways, to disabling power lines. It also includes direct confrontation with human offenders as you physically stop them from committing crimes against our fellow creatures.

As the name implies, **militant interventionism is an act of war against society**. It recognizes the liberators' passionate, forceful, and aggressive intervention into human oppression of our family. **Liberators use any and every tactic necessary to win the freedom of our brothers and sisters. This means they cheat, steal, lie, plunder, disable, threaten, and physically harm others to achieve their objective.**

Many compassionate people are probably reeling from this concept of militant interventionism. These are basically a peaceful people, opposed to violence. They ask whether militant interventionism lowers liberators to the level of the human oppressors. Can people lie, cheat, steal, and commit physical harm against others and call themselves moral persons?

Liberators contend that these questions ignore the difference between using physical force offensively versus defensively. They explain their position with the following example.

Stopping a would-be assassin from murdering an innocent child is considered, even by the most peaceful of us, to be a good, noble deed. Acting as an agent for the helpless child, it would be an act of defense, not offense. If the rescuer needed to lie, cheat, or steal from the would-be assassin, we would still praise his efforts. Lying, cheating and stealing are means of achieving the end of saving the child. Even if the would-be assassin was shot and killed to prevent him from killing the child, we would consider the rescuer praiseworthy and virtuous.

It should also be mentioned that liberators do not consider themselves punishers. They do not seek anything but the liberation of animals. If an abuser changes his or her behavior and adopts a peaceful lifestyle, liberators hold no grudges. What they do not accept is current crimes against members of our family. While some abusers could plead ignorance or habit, and while some people have the capacity to change, the fact remains that our fellow creatures are being tortured and slaughtered directly or indirectly by these people. Such crimes would not be tolerated by society if they were committed against humans. Liberators feel the same accountability must exist in the treatment of all creatures.

The fact that liberators are at war means that they use whatever force they feel is necessary to save our family members. They know that people, including the most bloodthirsty criminals, are never totally good or evil, black or white. But that fact never stopped people from killing criminals in self defense. **Liberators are not judging people as evil, but their acts as such. If people engage in the torture and destruction of innocent creatures, their acts make them guilty of crimes against other creatures, and liberators will try to stop them, even if that requires physical intervention. To stop the acts liberators feel they must stop the people. And the way liberators stop people is by using the motivations of pain and fear.**

Some of you may believe that force will never work in teaching people to respect animal life. Liberators agree. That is not their goal, however. **Liberators are not trying to educate humans. They have given up on humans and their societies. Militant interventionism is an approach that capitalizes on the motivation of pain and fear in making people act in certain ways.** When liberators give pain to vivisectors, or hunters, or fur farm breeders, or butchers, they make their oppression of animals less pleasurable. Some abusers will stop what they are doing. Of course, some will get guns and try to defend themselves. A high level of anxiety will be generated by liberations, which can also be used against the abusers. The more difficult and painful liberators make abusers' acts of brutality, the more it helps our family members.

Let me illustrate militant interventionism in action, in contrast to traditional methods of working within the system. Consider ways in which to handle vivisection.

Animal defenders stand with banners outside of a research facility, chanting: "What do we want? Animal Rights! When do we want it? Now!," as media people interview the leader or spokesperson. Across from them is an animal research support group, consisting of graduate students, researchers, and their children. They chant slogans back at the media, and are equally represented on the six o'clock news that evening. An article in the newspaper describes the demonstration, quoting the parts of the animal rights spokesperson's statements that sounded most "terrorist-like," since the public likes an exciting story. A well respected researcher at the facility is also quoted, as he explains to the public that animal research is critical for public health, and if animal research had not been allowed these activists would probably not be alive today. Meanwhile, behind the research facility's eight foot fence and barbed wire, behind the brick walls and metal cages, our family members crouch in fear, pain, and terror. They didn't even get to see the nice demonstration on television.

Some activists go home from the demonstration eager to write their Congressmen, asking for better conditions for lab animals and more strict regulations of research labs. But the Congressmen are lobbied more vehemently, and more effectively, by special interests groups invested in animal research, like the powerful pharmaceutical, medical, animal breeding, pet food, and meat industries. The fur, leather, and other animal abusing industries also lobby hard in favor of animal research, since they see any sign of respect for animals a dangerous precedent that might affect them as well. Some of the letters to Congressmen ask for enforcement of already passed laws, since enforcement is an entirely different matter than getting laws passed. So the animal defenders are left asking for laws to enforce the law. Of course, if successful, they will then need to ask for laws to enforce the enforcement laws.

Alternatively, imagine a liberator engaging in militant interventionism. The research facility is carefully staked out. Infiltrators give information about the locations of accessible animals. One night a break-in is attempted, and twenty rabbits, forty mice, six dogs, and two chimpanzees are rescued. Machinery used in experiments is destroyed, along with expensive computers and other valuable items. The animals are transported to sanctuaries where they can live out the rest of their lives in peace. Meanwhile, the police are busy looking for clues to the "crime". Researchers speak to the public about their outrage over the theft of their animals and the destruction of their property, and how medical science has just suffered a grave setback.

Then, one day, one of the animal researchers receives a letter asking him to stop his work or suffer the consequences. Of course, the researcher continues his cruel work. A week later he gets into his car and it explodes, permanently putting an end to his projects. Other researchers receive anonymous letters telling them to stop killing animals or they, too, will be stopped.

As a result, private and public police protection is ordered for the researchers. The facility looks like a fortress. Morale at the facility is low.

Researchers feel unsafe even at home. Some decide to retire early, or leave to another facility. A few of the graduate students and researchers' children decide that animal research is too dangerous for their blood, and choose to pursue another career. Soon, the cost of hiring private police protection reduces the amount of research that the facility can afford to conduct, and the public begins to get angry at the facility for using tax money to pay for public police protection.

We have thus considered two scenarios in dealing with vivisection. In one, letters were written, speeches were made, papers were sold, the public was momentarily amused, and animals still suffered and died. In other, animals were liberated, a chronic animal killer was neutralized, and terror, demoralization, and financial pains hampered further animal suffering (of course, I, Screaming Wolf, do not support this or any such fictitious scenario due to its illegality).

When people say this sounds like too much involvement for them, liberators ask them to consider what they would say if it was their family in that facility who was about to be tortured and slaughtered. Would they be standing outside chanting and writing to Congressmen, or would they be doing everything they possibly could to stop the bastards from killing their family?

Liberators contend that if you could imagine yourself doing this for your human family, then you should be able to imagine yourself doing it for your family of creatures.

Liberators capitalize on the fact that death threats, occasionally carried out, can demoralize more than researchers. Drug company executives, factory farmers, animal breeders, slaughter house workers, pet store owners, loggers, trappers, hunters, and every other abuser of animals are targets for militant interventionism. Imagine the difference between sabotaging a hunt by making noise to frighten away animals, and sabotaging a hunt by posing as a hunter and blowing away a real one. **Liberators commit themselves to making animal abuse a less pleasurable and more painful enterprise.**

Liberators offer guidelines for militant interventionism. This is how they explain their philosophy to interested individuals. I quote them for realism purposes, without implying any agreement with their principles. The following was delivered anonymously to me on cassette tape.

*"To begin with, **not everyone is capable of militancy.** Humans are taught to be compliant and unempowered. They fear direct action. If that is your situation, but you still believe in the liberation cause, then withdraw from the system. Do not participate in animal bloodshed or give society the*

benefit of your raised consciousness. Withdrawing from society saves lives, and bleeds the system of the good people it needs to go on living, and killing.

But if you feel you can practice militant interventionism, we suggest the following :

*First, **participate as little as possible in society.***

It is morally imperative that you participate in the cruelty of society to the least degree possible. We cannot accept the approach of killing some innocent creatures to save others. You wouldn't kill your brother to save your sister. If you could totally withdraw from society you could minimize participation in its cruelty. But since you have chosen to fight the system to liberate animals, you must participate in that system to some extent. Guns, nails, explosives, ski masks, and the transportation of you and the animals you save all cost money. Money is the medium of the society. You are therefore making a conscious choice to participate in some of the cruelty to stop some of it.

This sounds like a moral dilemma. How can you free the animals but not be a party to killing them by your participating in the system?

The answer is that the animals who are being destroyed covertly by your participation in the system, say, by your buying gasoline, driving your car, and paying sales tax for materials you could not steal, are like innocent captives of an armed, murderous terrorist who is about to kill them. The terrorist holds a child closely to his side as protection, as a shield. The only way to stop the terrorist from killing the other innocent captives is by killing the child along with him. You cannot see any other way of saving the others or the child. They will all die without your intervention. In this case, you must kill the terrorist and the child, saving as many other innocent victims as you can.

This is essentially the reality facing our family members. They are captives to human terrorists. *If we do nothing, all will suffer and be killed. So long as our participation does not add to the suffering they would have experienced without our intervention, we have done well.*

Clearly, then, we must participate in society only to the extend necessary to carry out our campaigns of liberation. *Any other involvement for personal gain would be losing our moral right to call ourselves liberators.*

*Second, **barter with other liberators and people who have withdrawn from society for essential needs.***

This rule follows from the first. Liberators can benefit from being in the company of like minded souls. In such a situation, people can share material objects and services by bartering with one another. This avoids having to go into town to buy the things you need. Try not to use money if at all possible.

Third, **make as little money as possible to get by.**

You may need some money to get things you can't barter for. Be careful! Making money is participating in the system. On the other hand, it could benefit the cause if you make money as an infiltrator, say, at a research lab or factory farm. How about getting a job as a security guard or janitor? They get lots of keys!

Fourth, **live simply.**

Avoid the obsession with materialism that plagues our capitalist world. We are raised to be consumers. The planet needs more liberation and less consumption. Living simply also helps you avoid needing money and having to participate in the system.

Fifth, **don't play by society's rules.**

Lie, cheat, steal, and do physical damage to abusers and their property, but do it if, and only if, it serves the needs of liberating our family from human tyranny. Do not break laws out of mere defiance or personal gain, for that robs you of your moral position, and it places you in unnecessary risk of getting caught.

It is worth mentioning here that liberators practicing militant interventionism do not take credit for their actions. We are not soldiers dressed in uniform facing the enemy head on. We are more like guerrilla warriors, spies and saboteurs. This is not a time for self-glorification and proving to the world that we are virtuous and brave. We do not need to sign our names or give our organizational affiliation, as the A.L.F. does. All pro-animal groups even the A.L.F., are trying to educate society and raise attention to their cause. They also want the opposition to know how strong and powerful they are. This is because they are struggling for power within the system.

Liberators have an entirely different agenda. We do not want the media to announce our actions, since that might make future actions more difficult. (An exception is when the media can add to the abuser's paranoia or serve as a tool of sabotage.) We do not want to educate society, since we know that society will never change. We do not want to be included in the power structure of the system. We simply want to liberate family members and *monkey wrench the abusive machinery of the system.*

*This difference pertains to acts of civil disobedience, as well. Civil disobedience, as discussed in the previous chapter, involves obeying all moral laws, and gladly accepting the punishment for disobeying immoral laws. It is designed to demonstrate your willingness to participate in society and obey its rules, so long as they are moral ones. Liberators, on the other hand, recognize that society is immoral and corrupt throughout, drenched with the blood of our fellow beings. We want nothing to do with society, except to sabotage its killing ability. **Civil disobedience makes no sense for liberators. It is not an appropriate tactic for war.***

The fact that we do not announce our activities adds to the terror and insecurity we can create, making us more effective. So long as vivisectors, for example, know that we are after them, that we will attack them at some time, in some manner, but that the time is for us to decide, and further, that we will never admit when we have attacked, we will have a ripping, destructive, demoralizing effect on the paranoid minds of these abusers. Was that open cage the act of a liberator? How about that new researcher who just started? Is he possibly an infiltrator? And how about that fire at Dr. Jones' house? Its cause never was completely determined.

A guilty mind needs no accuser. Abusers know who they are and will be fearing our every move. Whenever something bad happens, whenever someone is killed, or property is destroyed, or a car goes over a hill, or a person is poisoned when eating meat, liberators will be suspected. With nobody taking the blame abusers will not know who to trust. They will begin to turn on one another. We can thus demoralize them and hamper their oppression. Remember, fear is the greatest motivator of humans. We can generate an environment of fear that will singe the back hairs on even the most bloodthirsty oppressor.

*Sixth, **never trust humans without good cause.***

Remember, this is a war, and humans are the enemy.

This also means that you should work alone or with one or two other tried and true friends. People have been known to turn on even the closest friends with little apparent provocation. The war you are fighting might provide life and death reasons for others to turn on you.

It also implies that liberators have no leader. We are not organized in the traditional sense of the word. We are independent people accepting the responsibility of freeing our family members from human oppression. We don't take responsibility for one another's actions. We are empowered to do our own actions in accordance with our own conscience.

Seventh, **keep quiet about your beliefs.**

Loose lips can get you in deep trouble. Other good people will receive the message of liberation without your being the one telling them. You don't have to be a recruiter as well as a liberator. Lie about your beliefs, and be sneaky in your operation.

Eighth, **wean yourself from needing approval from other humans.**

You don't need people to tell you what a good job you are doing. Not many people are going to congratulate you for trashing a fur store and shooting a hunter, except maybe another liberator. Feel your success in the freedom and pleasure of liberated animals.

Ninth, **keep focusing on the positive.**

This one is a tall order. How can you go through life knowing the enormous cruelty that exists, and somehow maintain a positive attitude?

The answer is to realize that you have no control over that cruelty. As we have said, when you are in a burning house, it makes no sense to cry over the fact that the house is on fire. You must spend your energy on saving those who you can from the blaze, and expect that there will be many more who you cannot save. You must learn to see the blaze as the given, and your rescue of innocent victims as a boon.

Another way of saving this is using the analogy of a cup with water. You are familiar with the question of whether a cup containing half its maximum volume of water is either half empty, or half full. The optimist sees the cup as half full, the pessimist as half empty. **When you hope to rescue all of the animals and stop all human cruelty, you are choosing impossible goals. Your cup will always be half empty.**

But when you give up on unrealistic goals, you can feel good about every life you save that would have been destroyed without your intervention. Your cup is then half full. *But even half full is unrealistic, since it still judges your success by some ideal goal of freeing all our family members. In reality, a half filled cup is as full as it is ever going to get.* **You must learn to see each liberation of an animal as your cup running over.**

Another obstacle to feeling positive is that working within the system, which you may have been doing until now, seems trivial and impotent when you realize that animals need liberation, not rights. When you realize that *people are thick-headed, cruel beasts, and that the system is entrenched from top to bottom in animal exploitation, the old tactics of writing Congressmen, or getting a legislative initiative to stop pounds from selling dogs to animal research facilities, seem trivial. You now see that **Congress was made to serve men, not animals.** And you know that saving pound dogs from research facilities will only get those dogs killed at the pound, and force the researchers to buy more expensive dogs from breeders.*

It is true, however, that writing Congressmen is useful in that it costs oppressors of animals more money for their lobbying efforts. And the more spent on bred dogs, the less money available for research. But you now realize that these activities, even if successful, are simply temporary annoyances to abusers, and are ineffective in the long run. Businesses and researchers spending more money on operating costs will pass on their expenses to their consumers, many of whom are the animal defenders working within the system.

When you see the big picture, you have difficulty being satisfied with old, ineffective tactics. What you need to do is see the big picture from each animal's point of view, not from a human's. From their points of view, they are suffering and being killed. It's a life and death issue. Every time you liberate one from human tyranny, you are dealing successfully with their big picture.

In short, we cannot stop vivisection, but we can stop a vivisector. We cannot end hunting, but we can put an end to some hunters. We cannot cripple the fur industry, but we can cripple some trappers. We cannot put a halt to cars and trucks disabling animals, but we can disable cars, trucks, and roads.

So long as you are saving animals, you are winning wars! And winning wars should keep you feeling positive." These are the basic guidelines for militant interventionism as explained by liberators in their own words. Liberators feel it is a broad enough tactic to allow practitioners to pick a comfortable target and achieve their objective. For ideas, they suggest readers obtain a copy of *Ecodefense: A Field Guide to Monkeywrenching, Second Edition*, edited by Dave Foreman and Bill Haywood, and published by Ned Ludd Books, Tucson, Arizona, 1987. It is a "how to" guide for sabotage, and liberators believe it is easily applied to animal liberation.

Rather than adhering to any particular form of sabotage, liberators suggest that people be creative.

For example, they suggest people might use a rubber snake, or some other reptile facsimile, put nails throughout its body positioned in such a way that a car tire running over the snake would be flattened, and place the object on the road. Liberators say you'd be amazed how many people go out of their way to hit a snake. But this is one snake that the liberators hope will bite back!

Liberators might send bomb threats to universities and research facilities which use animals. If the person sending the bomb hasn't the inclination to carry out the threat, they suggest he or she ask a trusted and willing friend to do it, which will make future threats more effective.

They suggest people could buy a semi-automatic rifle and hunting license and go into the woods during hunting season to bag a "pot-bellied beer sucker". Or they might leak information to the media that some meat purchased at the grocery store was tainted with cyanide.

Liberators say that the possible projects are limited only by one's imagination. As they said at the end of the tape: *"Be careful, have fun, feel the goodness of what you are doing and kick some butt!"*

Liberators believe that people will discover, as they insist they have, that one can find happiness in this crazy world living the life of a liberator. In the next chapter I will discuss how liberators suggest that others can join their cause, and will examine the obstacles people may have to joining them.

Chapter Seven

FINDING PEACE IN TIMES OF WAR

Some of you may be agreeing with the liberators' assessment of human nature, society, and the inadequacy and inappropriateness of non-violent resistance for the liberation movement. You feel connected, as they do, to other beings in our family of creatures. You feel you must do something to defend your family. But the methods of liberation, withdrawing from society or staying marginally in society to engage in militant interventionism, are too difficult for you to fully practice at this time, even though you agree with them in principle. You don't want to be part of the problem, but you can't yet see yourself as part of the liberator solution, which is waging war with humans and their society. What do the liberators say you can do?

This is a good time to ask a difficult question. If liberators believe that humans are irrational, inconsistent, cruel, near-sighted, greedy, barbarous, alienated from themselves and nature, and covered from head to toe with the blood of innocent beings, what makes liberators believe that they are an exception?

The fact is, liberators recognize that they are no different. They, too, are human, and accept that they suffer from the human condition. They see themselves as products of society, social creatures who are an integration of culture and nature. But it is not a black and white situation. **When it comes to assessing one's involvement in human cruelty and the bloodshed it causes, liberators believe there are many shades of red.**

As the liberators see it, the **hunter** who seeks out life to kill is deeply red. So is the **researcher**, and the **drug manufacturer**, and the **slaughter house worker**, the **trapper** and the **furrier**, and the **fisherman**, and the **breeder**, and the **pet shop owner,** and the **highway driver**. The list is as long as there are people in society. **Everyone who participates in the cruelty of society bears the stigma of its bloodletting.**

Clearly, as far as the liberators are concerned, a vegan who doesn't drive, makes so little money that she pays no income taxes, and spends her time rescuing animals from local farms is a lighter shade of red than an animal researcher who hunts on weekends, eats meat, and pays thousands in taxes to support the killing machine.

When you chose to participate in society, even to liberate animals through militant interventionism, you are a shade of red. Even withdrawing from society does not cleanse you of redness. Withdrawal is a matter of degree. When you withdraw you take with you something from the cruel society, whether it be supplies or information. As a cultural animal, society is with you wherever you go. It affects the way you act, think and feel.

On a more tangible note, liberators point out that when you withdraw from society you are going to be living on somebody's land. If it is your own, you will have to pay taxes on it. If it is forest service or private land, you will probably have to deal with officials. The days of Walden Pond, where Thoreau left civilization, are over. In fact, Walden Pond is now a State run facility, and you have to pay a few bucks to go to its beach.

The fact that perfection is difficult to achieve, however, does not mean that it should be discarded as a goal. Liberators criticized Gandhi for relying on super-human Satyagrahis for his non-violent revolution. It could be argued that they, too, are demanding super-human dedication, clarity and commitment to be a liberator. But they realize that few people can be committed to a consistent moral position and make the types of deep sacrifices they are recommending.

Liberators suggest that we be realistic. Most people, even the most committed ones, are going to have difficulty withdrawing from society to the greatest extent possible. Few people will take their children out of school and leave for the forest to be self-sufficient survivalists, even though such a life would be more natural and healthy, not to mention more ethical.

But, as liberators see it, this is the **beginning** of the liberation movement. As the few people who are willing to make a sacrifice of their material and social comforts leave for the wilderness, small communities will form. It will become progressively easier for people to leave society as these communities develop.

The fact is, people need other people. We are social beings. Yet, because of our sensitivities to nonhumans, we feel disgusted and alienated from others who blindly practice the culture of cruelty. Many people feel, as liberators do, like aliens from another planet whenever they are out in society.

There are times when we feel like we have stepped out of reality and into the Twilight Zone, as when we go to shopping centers and see them filled with blank-faced, mindless consumers, or when we see restaurants lining the city streets selling the flesh of slaughtered creatures. The fact that people can live in urban settings, with traffic jams, pollution, overcrowding, rampant consumerism, and the total destruction of the natural environment and its replacement with asphalt and high rise buildings, is testimony to human alienation from nature. Humans are even alienated from their own natures as animals. We wonder how people can live such a life. As we reflect on this insanity, we feel alone in the world – **like millions of other people!**

Because of our social natures, however, our distaste for other people and our alienation from them and their culture does not stop us from feeling a need to be among them to some extent. How do liberators resolve this ambivalence?

They realize that they are not alone in their alienation from the insanity of others. Even now, communities exist in the forests and mountains where people have withdrawn from society to the greatest extent possible and live a natural life among other like-minded souls. They have discovered that they did not need to sacrifice their sensibilities for human companionship.

In truth, such a sacrifice is useless. When we give up our sensibilities to be with alien people, we become alienated from ourselves, and loose all chances of finding fulfilling companionship. Remember, the basis for enjoying others is the ability to find empathy with them. You can't empathize with aliens, because, by definition, aliens are those with whom you do not identify, and identification is the basis of empathy. You are only wasting your time with people whom you cannot relate to.

Let me illustrate this dilemma with a common example. As a vegan, you feel anxious every time your family invites you over for Thanksgiving. You know that a member of your wider family, a turkey, will be slaughtered, disemboweled, beheaded, plucked, cooked, and eaten for this occasion, and you want no part of it. To make you happy, the hosts have made some vegetables for you to eat. They expect you to be content sitting with them as they devour the turkey, as long as you can eat your vegetables. They expect you to respect their behaviors as long as they respect yours.

Some people submit themselves to this abuse each year in the name of civility, friendship, or family loyalty. Of course, as far as the turkey is concerned, you are not being civil, friendly, or loyal. **To liberators, it is all human-centered bullshit!**

Other people have declined such invitations, choosing to feel lonely rather than disgusted.

Still others have realized that there are other vegans with the same feelings of alienation who would love to get together. There is nothing so wonderful as eating a vegan meal with other vegans, when you finally feel a connection to other humans. Such community feeling is happening in the liberation movement, even in the wilderness. Liberators suggest you keep your eyes and ears open for others with like mind.

Liberators, then, believe that people can withdraw from society without having to miss quality human companionship. It's just a matter of finding the right, like-minded people. As for militant interventionism, liberators suggest that people who currently decide to stay within society can capitalize on their situation and become saboteurs. A committed individual can lower his or her standard of living in order to consume as little as possible, can drive as seldom as possible, and can eat a vegan diet. This will lighten their shade of red. As far as liberators are concerned, acts of militant interventionism, from a brick through a pet store window and the liberation of animals, to the slashing of animal transport vehicle tires, will lighten their shade even further.

Two people who read this book and agree with its principles can work together, recommend liberators. One can work as an infiltrator in a lab, or a slaughter house, or a grocery store, and feed the other information for militant intervention. If someone makes more money than they need, liberators suggest that they can support someone else who wants to spend all of his or her time in sabotage.

What liberators believe this shows is that people can participate in the liberation movement without needing to be perfect human beings. Realizing that we are not perfect is like realizing that we cannot change society. It makes no sense to lament what we can not be; but we can find optimism and hope in realizing what we can become. Liberators hope we, too, can engage in animal liberation to the greatest degree possible, all the time trying to become more consistent, more militant, and further removed from society. **According to liberators, we can all engage in the life long process of becoming a lighter shade of red.**

But what about the multitudes of people who feel sympathy for the liberation position, but simply oppose any form of force against humans? The majority of people who care for animals are simple, compassionate folks, wanting to make the lives of animals more pleasant at the hands of human tyrants. They are never going to drop out of society, break the law, or even go to a rally against vivisection or fur. They will, however, send money to animal groups, treat their pets well, and feel guilty every time they eat a steak. These people are the bread and butter of the animal defender constituency. What role do liberators see these people playing?

This is an important question. **The fact is that few people will take up the life of a liberator. Liberators hope that those who do not join them can at least admit to themselves that such a life, with its strategies of withdrawal and militant interventionism, is the most consistent position to take if one wishes to live as a true animal defender, and the most effective method for liberating our family of creatures from human oppression.** If they admit this to themselves, and consider the liberation ethic an ideal, liberators hope they can also admit it to others. At the very least, **they can stop condemning liberation activities, such as**

Animal Liberation Front raids, as unacceptable acts of "terrorism".

This is a real issue that is currently splitting the animal defense movement. Most large animal organizations are quick to condemn A.L.F. raids in the hope of maintaining an air of respectability. They know that A.L.F. activities cause the public, the opposition, and the media, to paint the entire movement with one brush, calling all animal defenders "terrorists". Knowing that moderate members, like the ones just described who oppose illegal activity of any sort, will stop sending donations to groups which support such activities, these groups are eager to take a loyalty oath to society and denounce any illegalities committed in the name of animal liberation.

A.L.F. activities are not only to be praised, according to the liberators, but the people doing these raids should be encouraged to be more confrontational and destructive to oppressive humans, a position which the A.L.F. publicly denounces. Liberators hope to persuaded all those who wish to engage in A.L.F. activities to practice militant interventionism in a broader form.

It is not the liberators' intention to belittle people who cannot accept the full commitment of becoming a liberator. Their premise that people are extremely imperfect demands that they be sensitive to human frailty. **People participating in the system are a darker shade of red than a liberator. The liberators state that they can slightly compensate for their participation by assisting the liberation movement as much as possible.**

These people, according to liberators, can influence that 12% of the public who care about ethical issues, but would be alienated by the more rigorous and extreme position of the liberator. People change slowly, and there is a place in the movement for people to assist others in moving towards a liberation ethic. The more people who become sympathetic to the liberation cause, the more the animals will be helped.

This means that standard tactics of writing to Congressmen, holding a rally, writing letters to the editor, and talking with friends, fellow workers, and family, have their place in the eyes of liberators. These tactics will not free animals, but they will cause the oppressors some grief as they scramble to maintain control over consumer's behaviors.

Remember, according to liberators, trying to improve the moral fiber of society is a lost cause. Efforts must be focused on monkey wrenching the abusive system, creating obstacles to oppression. Anything that causes the animal abusers difficulty in carrying out their oppression is a good deed.

Spending money on lobbyists, television commercials, and lawyers makes animal abuse more painful and less rewarding.

In other words, **these standard tactics are annoyances to the powerful abusers, not a prevention of their activities. There is no way to stop them on a large, societal scale. But liberators feel they can stop them on a small, individual scale.** To do this they believe they must practice militant interventionism.

Their position on non-violent tactics is that they work minimally, but are better than nothing. However, they should not be used with the hope of transforming society. They believe that no one will ever change society in any meaningful way in favor of animal respect. **Non-violent tactics should be used, say the liberators, with the intent of monkeywrenching the system, not changing it. The more people feel that non-violent efforts will change the system, the less willing they will be to revolt against it.** This is why liberators feel non-violence is dangerous if practiced for the wrong reason. False hopes that it can work will hurt the animals in the long run. It perpetuates a belief in the system and a commitment to working things out with abusive humans and their abusive social machine.

In short, liberators ask that animal supporters make their best contribution to the liberation movement, and support those who are willing to be extreme in their approach. Supporting them is supporting the animals that they are rescuing.

Liberators have a positive outlook about their work and their approach. They hope their positive outlook is contagious, for there is much to feel positive about. The motivation for their actions are based on their feelings, particularly their empathy for all beings in our family. Liberators are loving people. But **love does not have to be manifested only in our suffering for abused family members.** They can also have empathy for free, happy members. Empathy is a flexible tool for connecting with others. It allows us to feel another's pains or pleasures. As empathic beings, liberators feel they can also find true happiness in the world, even as they work to relieve suffering.

Put differently, the more pain you feel the more pleasure you can also feel. Empathy makes liberators passionate people. **They feel they can cry with the oppressed and laugh with the free.** An ability to empathize and feel a connection to others is essential for feeling love, since love is the ultimate form of connection. **Liberators say they do not have to limit themselves to loving only those who are suffering.**

The example they use to explain this is that, if you had many brothers and sisters, and some of them were being tortured and murdered, you would dedicate your life to liberating them, However, that would not limit you from receiving pleasure from the love for your other brothers and sisters who are free.

What this all boils down to is that liberators feel it is all right to enjoy life, despite the carnage that surrounds them. Liberators believe their empathy makes them capable of feeling true love. They claim that they are probably the most fulfilled, loving, self-actualized people on Earth.

For those willing to enter the process of becoming a liberator, liberators offer more words of encouragement.
These were included on the cassette.

"Your emotions are powerful, not only in making you receptive to love as well as suffering, but in sustaining your commitment to liberation. Many people are motivated by their heads. They have become so alienated from nature that they allow themselves to get caught up in mind games, and give their heads preference over their hearts. Hearts are intuitive, while the intellect needs reasons and explanations that intuition cannot provide.

These head trip people are the ones who read books like "Diet for a new America," by John Robbins, and intellectually appreciate the importance of becoming a vegan. They might even try it for a few weeks, or maybe even a few months, and then give up because it was too difficult to eat in restaurants, or because they really love eating turkey flesh on Thanksgiving and Christmas. Some will go back to eating meat when they read another book, by another self-proclaimed expert, telling them that meat is necessary for good health. Head trippers have no staying power. The mind is a fickle organ.

We do not expect head trippers to ever become liberators. It takes commitment and lots of heart to do our job. You may have the heart that it takes. Be proud of yourself and your ability to feel if you have this rare sensitivity.

*You might feel alone in your commitment to liberation. You are not. Realistically, we must expect that most people will resist the messages in this book. **People suck!** There's no getting around that fact. But there will be others like ourselves who will recognize these truths, and who will join our cause. Our numbers will always be few compared to the abusers and cowards. Our small numbers make each of us even more valuable and special. But our numbers will grow, as our efforts reinforce and validate others who feel the way we do. And many thousands of people feel as we do.*

106

The fact that we do not announce our activities as do standard groups makes our numbers uncountable. One liberator can seem like hundreds, as the paranoid minds of abusers reap the bitter harvest they have sown. Take pride in your courage, and feel confident in your effectiveness. The animals are benefiting from our efforts. To the liberated animal we mean the difference between life and death. Every liberator is a true hero."

This book was written to explain the intellectual justification used by those who believe in animal liberation. The issues are complex, as you have discovered. I have tried presenting them clearly and concisely. **Please reread this book, understand what has been said, and decide on its validity.**

Everyone reading this book is an animal abuser, according to the liberators. For that reason, if for none other, we should all be concerned about their message and approach. Chances are that violence will accelerate over the years as people become increasingly disenchanted working within the system. At the same time, the growing human population virtually guarantees increased animal abuse. The situation is becoming critical.

In the meantime, millions of our brothers and sisters are dying each day. Right or wrong, liberators have empowered themselves to do what they feel is right for our family. For them, the war has begun!

About The Author

I am sure that many of you would like to know who I am. My identity is something I expect to never reveal. Those who abuse animals for a living, or for pleasure, or just out of habit, will want to hunt me down to prove that they have the power to continue their oppressive lifestyles. Those who call themselves animal rights or welfare organizations will want to squelch my presentation of the liberators' condemnation of the human-centered status quo, in which they prosper. In short, I expect very few people will receive my words of truth with honest delight and acceptance.

In the event that someone tries to capitalize on my pseudonymous state and claims that he or she is Screaming Wolf, perhaps in an attempt to discredit my work, or to gain personal notoriety, please check with the publishers of this book. They do not know who I am at present, but I will reveal myself to them first, before any public statements are made. It is through them that I shall speak.

Original publisher's note: The text of this book was printed in the form in which it was received on a computer disk. No editing of its contents has occurred. All emphases are those of the author, Screaming Wolf. We are not responsible for its contents, and its publication is not meant as an endorsement of any of its statements, policies, or positions.

www.ingramcontent.com/pod-product-compliance
Lightning Source LLC
Chambersburg PA
CBHW050539280326
41933CB00011B/1641